Editor-in-Chief and Founder:
    Lyndon H. LaRouche, Jr.
Editorial Board: *Lyndon H. LaRouche, Jr. , Helga
    Zepp-LaRouche, Robert Ingraham, Tony
    Papert, Gerald Rose, Dennis Small, Jeffrey
    Steinberg, William Wertz*
Co-Editors: *Robert Ingraham, Tony Papert*
Managing Editor: *Nancy Spannaus*
Technology: *Marsha Freeman*
Books: *Katherine Notley*
Ebooks: *Richard Burden*
Graphics: *Alan Yue*
Photos: *Stuart Lewis*
Circulation Manager: *Stanley Ezrol*

INTELLIGENCE DIRECTORS
Counterintelligence: *Jeffrey Steinberg, Michele
    Steinberg*
Economics: *John Hoefle, Marcia Merry Baker,
    Paul Gallagher*
History: *Anton Chaitkin*
Ibero-America: *Dennis Small*
Russia and Eastern Europe: *Rachel Douglas*
United States: *Debra Freeman*

INTERNATIONAL BUREAUS
Bogotá: *Miriam Redondo*
Berlin: *Rainer Apel*
Copenhagen: *Tom Gillesberg*
Houston: *Harley Schlanger*
Lima: *Sara Madueño*
Melbourne: *Robert Barwick*
Mexico City: *Gerardo Castilleja Chávez*
New Delhi: *Ramtanu Maitra*
Paris: *Christine Bierre*
Stockholm: *Ulf Sandmark*
United Nations, N.Y.C.: *Leni Rubinstein*
Washington, D.C.: *William Jones*
Wiesbaden: *Göran Haglund*

ON THE WEB
e-mail: eirns@larouchepub.com
www.larouchepub.com
www.executiveintelligencereview.com
www.larouchepub.com/eiw
Webmaster: *John Sigerson*
Assistant Webmaster: *George Hollis*
Editor, Arabic-language edition: *Hussein Askary*

EIR (ISSN 0273-6314) *is published weekly
(50 issues), by EIR News Service, Inc.,
P.O. Box 17390, Washington, D.C. 20041-0390.
(703) 777-9451 ext. 415*

European Headquarters: E.I.R. GmbH, Postfach
Bahnstrasse 9a, D-65205, Wiesbaden, Germany
Tel: 49-611-73650
Homepage: http://www.eirna.com
e-mail: eirna@eirna.com
Director: Georg Neudecker

Montreal, Canada: 514-461-1557

Denmark: EIR - Danmark, Sankt Knuds Vej 11,
basement left, DK-1903 Frederiksberg, Denmark.
Tel.: +45 35 43 60 40, Fax: +45 35 43 87 57. e-mail:
eirdk@hotmail.com.

Mexico City: EIR, Sor Juana Inés de la Cruz 242-2
Col. Agricultura C.P. 11360
Delegación M. Hidalgo, México D.F.
Tel. (5525) 5318-2301
eirmexico@gmail.com

Canada Post Publication Sales Agreement
#40683579

Postmaster: Send all address changes to *EIR*, P.O.
Box 17390, Washington, D.C. 20041-0390.

Signed articles in *EIR* represent the views of the
authors, and not necessarily those of the Editorial
Board.

Cleaning Out 16 Years of Bush-Obama Filth

EDITORIAL

Lyndon LaRouche's Four Laws for Productivity

Nov. 24—LaRouche's Four Laws constitute one unified policy directed to the increase of human productivity.

Consider, for one central example, the unified international space program of the near future, in which a revived NASA will integrate its efforts with the leading role of China; with a revived Russian program based on the needed revival of Russian science; with Europe; and with many other countries just now beginning to look towards space. And soon, this world space-program will extend itself to incorporate the industrialization of the Moon, as the great Krafft Ehricke had forecast. Soon, scientific, engineering, and industrial activities on the Moon, will constitute a unique and irreplaceable part of the whole space program,— no longer only a world space program, but one already incorporating near-earth space as well.

Not only that: the crash program for fusion power which is LaRouche's Fourth Law, will itself be integrated within the worldwide space program. Human exploration of the Solar system requires fusion power, which in turn means that fusion power must be designed into the whole effort from the very beginning,—recall, for example, how all the features of the obsolete space system we have used up to this point, have all been shaped by the characteristics of the chemical propulsion systems used.

Study of the German, Russian, and U.S. ballistic-missile programs of the 20th Century, which preceded and laid the basis for the subsequent space programs, shows us history's largest-scale vertical and horizontal integration of the efforts of many thousands of people across numerous scientific, engineering and industrial disciplines and areas. And the required seamlessly integrated design, engineering, production, and testing, were all fundamentally based on new physical principles. They all culminated in a unique system,—never before seen,—incredibly complex, constituting thousands of parts, yet intolerant of even a single failure.

When the missile program transitioned over into the space program,— when mankind first stepped out into space beginning with the Soviets' launch of Sputnik in 1957,— the required

Official website of S.P. Korolov, RSC Energia
Cosmonauts V.F. Bykovsky (right) and V.V. Tereshkova, the first woman in space (left), welcomed after their flight by S.P. Korolov (center) and Yuri A. Gagarin.

scale and complexity required of the unified space effort, expanded beyond recognition, even when compared with the prior ballistic-missile revolution. For example, Boris Chertok, in his pioneering, first-person, four-volume history of the Soviet space program, wrote:

> I dare say that Korolyov [S.P. Korolyov, the greatest leader of the Soviet program] was perhaps the first to understand that space technology required a new organization.... For Korolyov, his deputies, and close associates, this gigantic new system came about because of a broad view of space technology, by combining fundamental research, applied science, specific design, production, launches, flight, and flight control, rather than from specific spacecraft. This single-cycle setup began to operate in 1959 and 1960. The mastery of this cycle by hundreds and later by many thousands of scientists and specialists, made it possible for humankind to begin the Space Age in the 20th century.

Top engineers and designers were to be seen in deep discussions with machinists on many of the shop floors; those engineers, in turn, regularly deliberated in committees, and in more intimate settings, with the most renowned leaders of theoretical science. The horizontal integration through dozens of institutes and factories was just as intense. It is amazing that this could ever happen under the Soviets' central-planning system,— that had required the hard school of World War II as a prerequisite,— but that is another story. But it all began to fall apart after a huge, tragic accident in 1960, and then the British Empire Thatcherite agents gutted everything that was left of Soviet science in the 1990s.

For the space program of the near future, what is needed is the Hamilton/LaRouche credit system, centered and steered by a National Bank, which is a flexible, universal system which supports all parts of this massively intricate chain of production, from top to bottom and from end to end, and which incorporates within itself what the late Charles de Gaulle called "indicative planning." And of course, we're not just talking about space travel here, but every color and flavor of increased human productivity.

Our most recent experience of this, is the means by which Franklin Roosevelt's application of Hamilton's credit system made the United States the Arsenal of Democracy for World War II, and the greatest economic power, by far, ever seen in the world. Loaning instant, low-interest money on contracts from the top to the bottom of the hierarchy of defense production, Roosevelt's system enabled this massive structure to "turn on a dime." To "turn on a dime" towards brand-new, just-introduced higher levels of science and technology. Just what we need now,— and what we must get through LaRouche's Four Laws

EIRContents

www.larouchepub.com Volume 43, Number 49, December 2, 2016

Cover This Week

National Archives/Gary Miller

I. A Future for Our Children

Xi Jinping's Ibero-American Tour Signals Global Strategic Shift

by Cynthia R. Rush

Nov. 28—On the eve of Chinese President Xi Jinping's Nov. 17 arrival in Ecuador for a state visit, that country's President Rafael Correa stated that Xi's visit "was the most important visit by a head of state in Ecuador's history," adding that China's involvement in Ecuador's economic development had "changed Ecuador's history" forever.

Also anticipating Xi Jinping's arrival, Chile's former ambassador to China, Fernando Reyes Matta, told Xinhua, "we will joyfully welcome Xi Jinping to Chile…We have new subjects [to discuss], new potentialities to dream, create and imagine with our feet placed in the 21st Century to develop both nations."

These remarks are emblematic of the breathtaking shift in the global strategic situation, including in Ibero-America, away from the rotting trans-Atlantic financial system and toward the Russia- and China-led New Paradigm of "win-win" cooperation, to transform the planet with massive infrastructure development and advanced science and technology. This is what Xi Jinping has repeatedly referred to, over the past few years, and in last week's Ibero-American tour, as building a "Community of Common Destiny."

The optimism and enthusiasm with which the Chinese President was greeted during his Nov. 17-23 state visits to Ecuador, Peru, and Chile, during which he outlined exciting proposals for broader cooperation at all levels, and the response to his crucial intervention at the Nov.

19-20 Asia-Pacific Economic Cooperation (APEC) summit in Lima, offered stunning confirmation of this shift in a region where, only three months ago, London and Wall Street financial predators were boasting they had taken back the region for "their" side, after staging a coup against Brazil's nationalist President Dilma Rousseff. That international bankers' coup was intended to pull Brazil out of the BRICS, of which it is a founding member, or greatly weaken its role.

The explosive response to Schiller Institute President Helga Zepp-LaRouche's keynote presentation at the Nov. 17-20 annual congress of the Economists Association of Peru, held in the Amazonian city of Pucallpa, was another powerful indicator of this strategic shift. Orga-

Xinhua/Lan Hongguang

Ecuador President Rafael Correa (second from right) holds a welcoming ceremony for Chinese President (center) at the airport in Quito, Ecuador, Nov. 17, 2016.

nized around the theme "The Peru-Brazil Bioceanic Train: Impact on the Economy of the Amazon Region and the Country," the conference heard Zepp-LaRouche speak on Nov. 17, the same day that Xi Jinping began his Ibero-American tour, on the subject of "the New Silk Road Concept: Facing the Collapse of the World Financial System."

The broad impact of her keynote—hundreds of DVDs of it are circulating widely— was such that in summarizing the results of the Pucallpa gathering, in a document sent out to 20,000 members, Roberto Vela Pinedo, the Dean of the Ucayali chapter of the Economists Association which hosted the national congress, pointedly wrote that "analyzing the keynote address presented to us by Dr. Helga Zepp-LaRouche, we share the perspective on world development that her message presented…" (See page 11.)

Xinhua/Ju Peng

Chinese President Xi Jinping (center) attends the 24th APEC Economic Leaders' Meeting in Lima, Peru, Nov. 20, 2016.

Center of Gravity Has Shifted

In a Nov. 20 discussion with associates, Zepp-LaRouche emphasized that these developments reflect the international shift in "the center of gravity and power" to the "new power center" located in the New Paradigm and China's One Belt, One Road initiative—a dynamic which has also been shaped by Lyndon and Helga LaRouche's own decades-long fight on behalf of the World Land-Bridge conception—which has evolved in accelerating fashion in a series of rapid-fire regional conferences in the past two months leading up to the APEC summit. The Sept. 2 meeting of the Eastern Economic Forum in Vladivostok was followed by the Sept. 4-5 G-20 meeting in Hangzhou, China, the Sept. 6-7 Association of South East Asian Nations (ASEAN) meeting in Laos and the Oct. 16 BRICS summit in Goa, India—all sharply focused on integrating the Eurasian Economic Union (EAEU) with China's One Belt, One Road initiative.

Today's reality, Zepp-LaRouche said, is that the "trans-Atlantic establishments are completely incapable of understanding that their model of globalization and neoliberal distribution of wealth from the poor to the rich has *completely failed,* and they are neither able to predict developments nor can they cope with the consequences of" such events as the June Brexit vote in Britain or the Nov. 8 election of Donald Trump in the United States.

APEC: Death Knell for the TPP

The APEC summit, and the bilateral meetings and discussion that took place around it, reflected this new global reality, starting with its delivering a well-deserved burial for Barack Obama's hideous Trans-Pacific Partnership (TPP), the bankers' corporate dictatorship disguised as a free trade agreement. While lame duck Obama couldn't even be bothered with addressing the summit—he was off trying to impress young Peruvians at a "town hall" meeting at Lima's Catholic University— Xi Jinping, Russian President Vladimir Putin, Philippine President Rodrigo Duterte, and other regional leaders seriously debated bold new initiatives to transform the Asia-Pacific region, a centerpiece of which is China's proposed Free Trade Area of the Asia-Pacific (FTAAP), first proposed at the 2014 APEC summit in Beijing.

In the past, Xi has used the annual APEC summits to launch major global initiatives. In 2014, aside from proposing the FTAAP, in a press conference with the hapless Obama standing at his side, he also announced the New Silk Road initiative and urged the United States and other nations to join in. Obama refused the offer. Then in 2015, in Manila, Xi announced the formation of the Asian Infrastructure Investment Bank (AIIB), again emphasizing it was open to the entire world. Obama turned his back on it. Now, in 2016, Xi is doing the same with the FTAAP.

Unlike the TPP, which was designed specifically to exclude China, the FTAAP would include all nations of the Asia-Pacific region wishing to join, including the United States, and is intended to foster the physical-economic development of the participating nations. As Xi emphasized in his Nov. 19 speech to the APEC CEO summit, the FTAAP "is a strategic initiative for the long-term prosperity of the Asia-Pacific," which is directly linked to the Belt and Road initiative which China proposed three years ago. "We need a framework of regional cooperation of equality, joint participation, and shared benefits. Arrangements that are closed and exclusive are not the correct option," he stressed. The "2016 Leaders' Declaration," issued at the end of the APEC summit, reiterates their "commitment to the eventual realization" of the FTAAP.

Xi stressed that over 100 countries and international organizations have joined in, or expressed support for, the One Belt, One Road initiative, forming "a close circle of friends brought together by the common vision, mutual trust and friendship." The AIIB, he said, "is up and running. The Silk Road Fund is in place ... China welcomes all parties to join this initiative to meet challenges, share opportunities and seek common development."

As he did at the early-September G-20 summit in Hangzhou, Xi stressed that the role of science and innovation is key, in solving the global economic crisis. "We will continue to pursue the strategy of innovation-driven development and deepen R&D structural reform to change outdated mindset and remove institutional obstacles, to fully leverage the role of science and technology in economic and social developments, and tap into all sources of innovation."

This is exactly what thinking Ibero-Americans want to hear.

'A Land of Vitality and Hope'

In what was clearly a coordinated move, just one day after Xi Jinping concluded his tour, on Nov. 24, China's Foreign Ministry issued a very detailed policy paper on China, Latin America, and the Caribbean, which it describes as a "blueprint for the future," based on "new ideas and proposals and initiatives" to deepen cooperation in a multitude of areas, including infrastructure building, technology transfer, manufacturing, science and technology, and aerospace, among others.

Describing Latin American and the Caribbean as "a land full of vitality and hope," the document states that China's relations with Latin America and the Caribbean are in "a new stage of comprehensive cooperation" at a time when the world is undergoing "unprecedented historical changes, with multipolarity and globalization gaining momentum."

The partnership among China, Latin America, and the Caribbean, it underscores, "is a shining example of developing countries working together to seek common development."

It is precisely this optimistic, future-oriented perspective to which Ibero-American leaders responded in the course of Xi's tour. In Ecuador and Chile, presidents Rafael Correa and Michelle Bachelet, respectively, signed agreements to upgrade their bilateral ties with China to the level of a "comprehensive strategic partnership," something already done by Peru during Chinese Premier Li Keqiang's May 2015 visit.

In both cases, that upgrade will mean expanded cooperation on several fronts, involving traditional areas such as mining, energy and agriculture, but also it is aimed at diversifying the relationship away from raw materials export and toward becoming partners with China, both in national industrialization plans and coordination in international affairs. Although the Obama Administration had strongly pressured Bachelet not to stray from the TPP, following her Nov. 21 meeting with Xi, during which they signed twelve cooperation agreeements, the Chilean President voiced support for the FTAAP—leaving the TPP issue hanging—and announced that her goverment wished to join the AIIB "as soon as possible."

Ibero-America Must 'Create Knowledge'

Science and technology are crucial components of these relationships as the Chinese Foreign Ministry document particularly emphasizes. As Chile's former ambassador to China Fernando Reyes Matta put it in a Nov. 17 statement to Xinhua, "it's time for Latin America and Chile to discover the meaning of the word 'innovation.'" The fundamental principles of China's development model, he said, "are related to the development of advanced science and technology." Latin America, he asserted, must develop "the ability to create knowledge."

President Correa was effusive in his praise for China in helping to finance his country's high-tech "City of Knowlege" located at Yachay, which he described as

chinca.org

The Coca Codo Sinclair hydropower project in Ecuador, begun in 2010, was built in four years by the Chinese Sino Hydro Group, and is the largest foreign investment— and on the largest-scale—of all that have been built or are under construction in Ecuador.

Ecuador's most important project, not because of its cost but because of its focus on the "hard sciences." (See page 12.)

In an interview with Xinhua published Nov. 20, President Bachelet stressed that "science, technology and innovation" are top priorities in Chile's bilateral relationship with China, and pointed to the importance of China's offers to help build various rail and other bioceanic corridors across South America—a subject she had also emphasized to Chinese Premier Li Keqiang during his May 2015 visit to Chile. In this context, she pointed to the possibility of connecting the two countries via an underwater fiber-optic cable, "which would be a bridge to the rest of Latin America…important for both countries' integration is what we can do in the Latin American region," she said.

Among the twelve agreements signed by Bachelet and Xi was one to set up a China-Chile agricultural research and development center. Chile is one of South America's premier agricultural producers, and both exports agricultural products to China and advises it on advanced agricultural techniques. Agriculture is a key component of the Peru-China relationship, as Xi mentioned. (See page 13.)

A highlight of Xi's two-day visit to Ecuador was the inauguration ceremony of major high-tech projects made possible by Chinese financing, including the emergency 911 system China had helped develop, and the giant Coco Coda Sinclair hydroelectric dam in Ecuador's remote Amazon region, built under Chinese engineering direction by a workforce of 7,000 Chinese

and Ecuadoreans. The project, which took six years to build and is the largest energy project in Ecuador's history, has a generating capacity of 1500 MW, and as one beaming official proudly announced, it is already exporting electricity to Colombia.

The two Presidents were also connected by interactive video to the groundbreaking (by huge excavators) for a new hospital in the city of Chone, whose old hospital was completely destroyed in the April 2016 earthquake. The head of China's CAMAC Engineering Co., which is in charge of the project, told the ceremony that CAMAC is committed to completing construction of the 120-bed hospital with state-of-the-art, earthquake-resistant technology.

Real 'Connectivity'

Premier Li Keqiang's May 19-26, 2015 trip to four Ibero-American nations—Brazil, Colombia, Peru, and Chile—focused heavily on construction of bioceanic corridors and was met with great exicitement, with one Peruvian commentary at the time describing the proposed Brazil-Peru transcontinental rail project, first put forward at the July 2014 BRICS summit in Brazil, as auguring the arrival of the New Silk Road to the Americas.

In a May 25, 2015 China-Chile Business Forum attended by Li, President Bachelet said "it is important to have China's support to attain the much-desired physical integration of South America through bioceanic corridors, in order to consolidate Chile's role as a port and bridge-nation looking toward Asia…we need important infrastructure works, both in the region and in Chile."

During Li's visit to Peru last year, a Memorandum of Understanding was signed by representatives of Brazil's Transportation Ministry, Peru's Transportation Ministry, and China's National Reform and Development Commission to begin the feasility study on the Brazil-Peru transcontinental railroad.

As just occurred in Peru with her Nov. 17 address to the Economists Association congress in Pucallpa, on May 28, 2015, two days after Li Keqiang completed his tour, Zepp-LaRouche delivered a strategic briefing on "The Silk Road Becomes the World Land Bridge" to an international video-conference in Lima, entitled "The BRICS Alternative and the Development of Peru and

South America," sponsored by the Association of Alumni of Peru's Superior War College (ADECAEM).

Joining Zepp-LaRouche as a speaker at that event was retired Chinese diplomat Dr. Liu Youfa, who emphasized the critical importance to Chinese-Ibero-American relations and their joint industrial development of building a transcontinental railroad, detailing the history of this "dream" which he said went back to South America's forefathers.

Today, while Peru's President and former Wall Street banker Pedro Pablo Kuczynski (PPK) insists he wants to expand trade with China, and signed agreements with Xi Jinping to that effect during their state visit, he has no intention of allowing the dramatic transformation of Peru's or South America's interior that building the Brazil-Peru transcontinental railroad would bring about. Although the feasibility study on the project was completed by the China Railway Eryuan Engineering Co. (CREEC) and delivered to the government, PPK is refusing to release it to Congress or other interested parties.

When he appeared before the press following his hour-long meeting with Xi and accompanying cabinet ministers Nov. 21, PPK reported on a number of agreements signed by the two, but *made no mention* of the Brazil-Peru bioceanic rail project. Nor did anyone else. (See page 15.)

But should he try to continue with his sabotage, PPK may quickly discover that history will pass him by, just as it is doing with Brazil's President Michel Temer or Argentina's London-owned President Mauricio Macri, who assume their loyalty to London and Wall Street means their futures are secure. In the context of the global strategic shift and support for China's "win-win" development cooperation, there will be no containing the repercussions of Helga Zepp-LaRouche's intervention at the Economists Association conference in Pucallpa, and the broad interest, press coverage, and spontaneous organizing activity it has unleashed.

Just one indication of that: Carlos Tubino, one of eight congressman from the opposition "Fujimorista" Fuerza Popular party (of former presidential candidate Keiko Fujimori) who attended a parallel event in Pucallpa, coinciding with the Economists congress, denounced sabotage of the bioceanic project as treason, and announced that upon his return to Lima, he will call a hearing of the congressional transportation committee on the Brazil-Peru rail project and demand that PPK's transportation minister appear for questioning.

Zepp-LaRouche Sparks Peru Mass Movement

Nov. 29—Few voices have ever been heard in any national conference of any economist associations in the trans-Atlantic region in recent decades discussing even the status of the existing physical economy, let alone a vision for its future development.

Not so in the XXIII Annual Congress of the Peru Association of Economists, held from Nov. 17-19. The Ucayali chapter of the national association, hosting this year's congress, organized the gathering around the subject of "The Peru-Brazil Bioceanic Railroad: Impact on the Economy of the Amazon Region and the Country," and they invited the world-renowned "Silk Road Lady," Schiller Institute founder and president Helga Zepp-LaRouche, to deliver the keynote presentation.

The Congress was held in Pucallpa, a city of some 210,000 people which is the capital of the department of Ucayali in Peru's Amazon region. The Ucayali economists have been in active discussions with several Chinese institutions on building the bioceanic train connecting the Atlantic and the Pacific through Peru and Brazil for good reason: Pucallpa is only an hour and 10 minute flight from the nation's capital, Lima, yet it takes two and a half *days* to reach Pucallpa by land, because of the condition of the roads leading to it. These folks understood that investment in infrastructure is required if any development is to occur.

Zepp-LaRouche presented the Economists congress, however, with a sweeping overview of the stunning potential for a New Paradigm for all of humanity, and what Peru's role can and should be in advancing it, which went far beyond the common, limited notion of infrastructure (see Nov. 25 *EIR*), and the effect was electrifying.

'Economy From the Moon'

"Congress of Economists Discusses a Futurist Plan of a Lunar Economy," *Impetu*, the "dean" of the Pucallpa media, headlined its coverage of the congress, featuring Zepp-LaRouche's presentation. Zepp-La-Rouche "argued that in less than a year, an alliance of nations has been created, which has built a parallel economy at breakneck speed dedicated exclusively to the building of the real economy, in opposition to the maximization of speculative monetary gain, which now includes more than half of humanity," *Impetu* wrote.

"This new community of nations"—Zepp-La-Rouche continued—"represents a center of power based on economic growth, and above all, on advanced technology which belongs to the future, as is seen in the success of the Chinese moon exploration program, focused on the idea of bringing great quantities of helium-3 from the Moon to Earth for the future thermonuclear fusion economy. She argued that this orientation for a futurist economy points the way to a scientific and technological revolution which will increase, by orders of magnitude, energy flux density, both in the production process on Earth, as well as in the fuel for space travel, and, in this way, introduce a completely new phase in the evolution of the human species."

Another Pucallpa daily, *Al Dia*, headlined its coverage: "Specialist Helga Zepp Explained Via Internet to the Congress of Economists that the Bi-oceanic Railroad Can Bring the World to a More Just Economic Order."

Zepp-LaRouche "explained that the bi-oceanic railroad is a project which will change the current world, which is seeking a more just economic order," they reported.

"She noted that the change of world paradigms, recently exemplified in the Brexit vote and the U.S. presidential elections, in the context of the global trans-Atlantic financial crisis, which is much worse than that of 2009, may have in the bi-oceanic railroad a basis for world economic recovery.

"Helga Zepp reviewed the history of China's 'One Belt, One Road' policy, the alternative to the trans-Atlantic financial collapse, as well as her own activity over 45 years, along with the U.S. economist Lyndon LaRouche, and with developing sector statesmen such as Indira and Rashid [sic] Gandhi and José López Portillo, among others, in support of development corridors designed to build a more just world economic order.

"Zepp-LaRouche's presentation shows the unique opportunity that the Brazil-Peru trans-continental rail project represents, which is being supported by broad political, business and professional sectors in Peru and South America, and by the Chinese government; whereas *The Economist* of London has attacked it as

EIRNS

Helga Zepp-LaRouche delivering the keynote to the 23rd National Congress of the Association of Economists of Peru on Nov. 18, 2016.

damaging to the Amazon 'environment,' a false and misleading argument, according to social organizations of the Peruvian Amazon region," the newspaper concluded.

A National Mobilization Begins

Zepp-LaRouche delivered her keynote address on Nov. 17, at the opening session of the congress. On the second day, a parallel meeting was held in Pucallpa to pressure for the immediate adoption of China's proposed Bioceanic Rail Corridor. More than 400 people attended this public session of the Transportation Committee of the National Congress of Peru, eight of whose members traveled from Lima to Pucallpa for the occasion. Numerous regional governors, including of the host region Ucayali, and mayors were also present, along with a number of popular organizations and business groups, as well as a strong delegation from the Association of Economists (whose national congress continued nearby). Peru's major national print and TV media were also present.

Hundreds of copies of a DVD of Zepp-LaRouche's presentation the day before, were handed out to those present by the head of the Ucayali Economists Association, as were hundreds of copies of the 60-page pamphlet published by the association, containing excerpts from *EIR*'s "The New Silk Road Becomes the World Land-Bridge" special report, and Lyndon LaRouche's Four Laws.

All of the congressmen present came out strongly in favor of the rail project, with a number of them denouncing the government of Pedro Pablo Kuczynski (PPK) for blocking the project. Congressman Carlos Tubino of the "Fujimorista" Fuerza Popular party (which was defeated in the recent presidential elections by Boston banker PPK), announced that, immediately upon his return to Lima, he would be calling a hearing in the national Congress on the rail project, and requiring the presence for questioning on the matter of PPK's Transportation Minister.

The Ucayali Development Front, a regional popular organization, spoke of organizing a regional strike if the rail project is not begun immediately. The Governor of Ucayali also spoke forcefully for the project. A detailed report on the technical details and feasibility of the project was given by Justo Vargas, an adviser to the Governor of Ucayali and a leading organizer of the Economists Association congress, who had also traveled to China earlier this year for meetings with CREEC (the China Railway Eryuan Engineering Group Company, Ltd.) and others. All in all, some 18 people—including *EIR*'s Peru representative Luis Vasquez—addressed the explosive meeting, of whom 16 voiced unqualified support for the project; only two raised "environmentalist" concerns.

'We Share Zepp-LaRouche's View'

Following the conclusion of the congress of the Economists, Roberto Vela Pinedo, Dean of the Association of Economists of Ucayali, issued a document summarizing the results of the gathering, sent to all 24 regional Associations of Economists in Peru with their 20,000 or so members. Its opening statement was blunt:

"We economists of Peru, gathered in the city of Pucallpa, informing national and international public opinion of our position regarding the current situation of the country and the world, state the following:

1) That, analyzing the keynote address presented to us by Dr. Helga Zepp-LaRouche, we share the perspective on world development that her message presented, and which can be seen at the following link: http://financiardesarrollo. blogspot.pe/2016/11/la-ferrovia-transcontinental-brasil.html "

After this opening point of emphasis, Vela went on to write:

"6) To overcome this crisis, the BRICS countries (Brazil, Russia, India, China and South Africa), led by China and Russia, proposed and initiated the construction of a new financial architecture directed at developing nations' physical economies, in a sovereign relationship in which everyone wins (the 'win-win' [original in English—ed.]) strategy, that demolishes the ancien regime's zero-sum game, under which some win and others lose… Peru must join this process in order to achieve growth.

7) We must restructure the state's economic policy and replace the neoliberal model with a model of development of productive transformation with equity…

8) We need to apply science, technology and innovation in our economic development, as the basis for being competitive…

11) We must create a Ministry of Strategic Planning to formulate the vision of the country we wish to be… and have a new Ministry of Technology and Production…

16) The first great step along the path of industrial development and the promotion of scientific and technological capabilities, is that Peru, as a paradigmatic example of this new sovereign relationship in which everyone wins (the 'win-win' strategy), should approve the proposal of the government of the Popular Republic of China to build a trans-continental railroad along the Northern Route, which would link the ports of Santos in Brazil and Bayovar in Peru, emphasizing the development of hundreds of complementary projects, such as: agriculture, agro-industry, manufacturing, fishing, ports, nuclear energy, petrochemicals, scientific and technological innovation, road infrastructure, the creation of new intelligent cities, and the creation of thousands of jobs, etc.

"After four days of deliberations, we have agreed to demand that the central government [of Peru] accept and promote the construction of this mega-project, given that it is the only one at this time focused on continental integration, and which already has a signed Memorandum of Understanding among the governments of the China, Brazil and Peru."

—*Gretchen Small*

China, Russia Foster Ibero-America's Scientific Development

Nov. 27—On the occasion of Chinese President Xi Jinping's state visit Nov. 17-18, Ecuadorean President Rafael Correa hailed China's financing of the Yachay "City of Knowledge"—Yachay is the Quechua word for "knowledge"—as "what I consider the most important project in our country's history, not because of its dollar amount, but because of its significance: the City of Knowledge, Yachay, which includes a world-class university, dedicated to fostering innovation and the development of the hard sciences."

China's Export-Import Bank, the China Gezhouba Group Company (CGGC), and the IZP Group are some of the Chinese entities building and financing the Yachay project which was launched in March 2014, and is the first *planned* city built in South America since the 1960 construction of Brazil's capital, Brasilia. China's backing, and more recently Russia's, is emblematic of these nations' commitment to cooperating with Ibero-American countries to accelerate their economic development by advancing their scientific and technological capabilities. Because Yachay is intended to serve as a regional hub for a variety of scientific, technological, and trade activities, China views it as a key component of the One Belt, One Road perspective.

Ecuadorean experts and participants explain that Yachay's goal is to create a new generation of scientists and engineers dedicated to building "a new economy based on knowledge, science and technology," the Andes news service reported last July. Many of the scientific, industrial, and agricultural entities operating there are directly linked to the im-provement of Ecuador's economy, and the benefits this will bring to its population, in terms of jobs, education, medical care, improved food production, and access to advanced technology.

In an August 2015 interview with Radio Universidad de Chile, Yachay's Technical Manager Fernando Cornejo emphasized the *international* nature of the project, with academics, students, and researchers from 54 countries involved. In addition to the Yachay Tech University, all of Ecuador's twelve national research institutes will be located there, along with an industrial park, the Superior Technological Institute, 37 high-tech companies, schools, hospitals, agro-industrial enterprises, and much more. The project, Cornejo underscored, is "an emblematic project of Unasur" (Union of South American Nations), designed to expand knowledge and development of science and technology throughout South America, to help it achieve its "second Independence."

Nor is China the only nation involved in Yachay. Russia's prestigious St. Petersburg Vaccine and Serum Institute announced Nov. 13 that it had signed an agreement with Ecuador's Foreign Ministry, to provide $30 million to build a vaccine and serum-production plant there, similar to the Mechnikov Vaccine Production Plant it has already built in Nicaragua. Russia provided $14 billion of Mechnikov's total $21 billion investment, offered technology, and trained Nicaraguan per-

Students working in the lab at Yachay University.

Carlos Silva/Vicepresidencia

sonnel at the St. Petersburg Institute. When fully operational in March 2017, the Mechnikov plant will supply vaccines not only to Central America and the Caribbean, but to other Ibero-American nations as well. The Yachay plant will supply both the domestic and regional market, and the St. Petersburg Institute has announced it will reinvest all profits in continued scientific research and development.

Bolivia also plans to build a "City of Knowledge" like Yachay in the city of Cochabamba, which is still in the planning stages, but has already gotten a financial commitment from China's Huawei Co. to build a laboratory that will train professionals and university students in telecommunications and information technology. Russia's nuclear energy agency, Rosatom, is also financing the construction of a state-of-the-art Nuclear Research and Development Center in La Paz that will benefit the entire region.

The Bolivian Public Works Ministry's official overseeing the Cochabamba project, Ariel Torrico, told the daily *El Dia* in a Nov. 1, 2015 interview, that the Cochabamba site will be a planned city from start to finish, to include all services and equipment "to house scientists, teachers and researchers." Areas of research include petrochemicals, agro-industry, information technology, telecommunications, alternative energy sources, and hydrocarbons, among others. With laboratories, housing, research and educational facilities, as well as recreational areas, the project aims to "exploit national knowledge to the maximum," Torrico said, "and prevent human capital from leaving the country," Torrico said.

Cornejo explained that the principle guiding the Yachay project is that *"we have changed the neoliberal conception of knowledge as a finite good, to one of knowledge as an infinite good that can be shared, is open and collaborative."* Knowledge, he continued, "is linked to independence." The challenge for Latin America, he said, is to transform itself into "a producer of knowledge." He emphasized that a project of Yachay's magnitude could only be carried out by the State, not the private sector. "It implied thinking big, in [terms of] megaprojects that would have a direct influence on the productive sector..." It also implied *"a change in the mentality of the Ecuadoreans and Latin Americans since a change in the productive matrix [of society] can only occur with a change in the cognitive matrix."*

—*Cynthia Rush*

Xi Commits to Enhanced Trade of Food, Ag R&D

Nov. 27—President Xi Jinping, in concluding his keynote to the APEC CEO Summit Nov. 19 in Lima, said, "We all know that the sweet potato and other varieties of potato originated in Latin America. I once used the sweet potato as an example to make a point to a group of Chinese business leaders. I said that the vines of sweet potato may stretch in all directions, but they all grow out of its roots. Similarly, no matter what level of development it may reach, China, with its root in the Asia-Pacific, will continue to contribute to its development and prosperity. China is committed to peaceful development and a win-win strategy of opening up...."

Not merely a nice metaphor for APEC, Xi's mention of the potato—which received a sudden, delighted applause—has literal meaning for win-win benefit to China and Peru. In recent decades, Peru—home of the potato—has supplied new varieties of potato to China, dramatically improving yields.

This in turn illustrates one part—R&D—of the two-fold content to the various new commitments on food and agriculture agreed to on President Xi's trip to Peru, Chile and Ecuador. The other part is expanded food trade.

Leaders in China and Chile are already very active in promoting agriculture science, and pledged to do more. There is a China-Chile demonstration project near Tianjin. New varieties of fruit trees, vineyards and agronomic practices are shown in action on a 23-hectare demonstration farm. Tourists, as well as scientists and farmers, are invited to enjoy the scenery and good food at the associated Andes International Resort.

For Chile, the Chinese Academy of Agricultural Sciences (CAAS) and the Institute of Agricultural Research of Chile intend to co-build an R&D center in Santiago, to collaborate in a number of areas. They include remote sensing applications, exchange of crop varieties, animal health and veterinary practices, and more.

The potato story between Peru and China is exemplary. Peru is home to the International Potato Center

Potato varietals in Peru.

(CIP), founded in 1971 as part of the world research network, the Consortium of International Agricultural Research Centers (CGIAR), instigated by Henry Wallace, Agriculture Secretary and Vice President under Franklin Delano Roosevelt. The potato originated in the Peru region, where its earliest cultivation goes back to at least 2500 B.C. Today, some 4,000 varieties (native and improved) are known. Among new strains developed by CIP is one called the Tacna, whose germplasm was provided to China in 1994. The Tacna was so well suited to northern China's dry, saline conditions, that it led to a 40% jump in China's potato output.

In Ecuador, Pres. Xi and President Rafael Correa agreed to explore cooperation in agriculture, along with energy and other areas, when they met Nov. 18, before the APEC Summit.

Besides research, commitments to enhanced trade were made for food and agriculture between China and the three nations on President Xi's tour.

In Chile, for example, food trade volume with China is already rapidly increasing. China is the third largest destination for Chilean food products (after the United States and Japan), and within 5 to 10 years Chile is expected to be first. A free trade agreement was struck 10 years ago between China and Chile, under which there are no tariffs on nearly 90% of food imports.

Chile, like California, has a wonderful Mediterranean agro-climate, favoring the production of hundreds of food products. Its major exports to China are table grapes, cherries, apples, kiwis, plums, and blueberries, besides being the second largest supplier of wine imports after France.

Ecuador, the world's largest source of banana exports, supplies China. Peru, under new trade standards reached with China since 2015, now supplies asparagus, avocadoes, and other foods.

The prospect here is for a win-win approach, for collaborative government action aimed at raising living standards and productivity through R&D and trade, for both Asia and South America.

This is in direct contrast to the lose-lose model imposed for the last 50 years of deregulated food trade under the domination of London and Wall Street. Under this destructive, neoliberal model, tariff-free entry into the United States allowed for Trans-Atlantic-based mega-food processors and distributors—e.g. Green Giant, Del Monte, Dole, Walmart et al.—to relocate food-sourcing (for many crops easily produced in the United States—peas, avocadoes, asparagus, etc.) in Peru, and elsewhere, by means of imposing conditions of cheap labor, cheap land use, and cheap processing. This has caused impoverishment both in Central and South America, and also in the United States, where thousands of family farms were put out of operation. Emblematic, is that the United States has even become a net importer of such an easily grown food as onions! Thus, Central, South American and Mexican farm potential has been subverted into national food export-dependency.

China has defined a different approach to the Americas in its new *Policy Paper on Latin America and the Caribbean*, released Nov. 24. Its sub-section, titled, "Agricultural Cooperation," states, in full:

"Efforts will be made to encourage enterprises on both sides to actively engage in agricultural trade, push for further exchanges and cooperation in agricultural science and technology, personnel training and other fields, deepen cooperation in livestock and poultry breeding, forestry, fishery, and aquaculture, and jointly promote food security. China will continue to set up and improve agricultural technology demonstration programs, promote the development and demonstration of modern agricultural technologies, and enhance agricultural technology innovation, agricultural production, and processing capacity and international competitiveness on both sides. Bilateral mechanisms for agricultural information exchanges and cooperation will be improved while giving full play to the role of the special fund for China-Latin America agricultural cooperation, and more agricultural cooperation projects are encouraged."

—*Marcia Merry Baker*

South America's Transcontinental Railroad

Nov. 27—The single most important Great Project that the Chinese government of Xi Jinping has put on the table for South America, that of construction a "bioceanic rail corridor," a transcontinental railroad from Brazil's Atlantic coast to Peru's Pacific coast, was not mentioned even once, publicly, during Xi's Nov. 19-21 visit to Peru, including during his participation in the APEC summit in Lima and his state visit and meeting with Peruvian President Pedro Pablo Kuczynski. But the rail project was the proverbial "elephant in the living room" which dominated all of the proceedings—even though no one mentioned it.

That is because a South American transcontinental railroad is a total game-changer—and friend and foe alike know it. Its physical economic impact cannot be measured in track-miles built; tons of cargo transported; jobs created; trade with Asia multiplied; or even square kilometers of South America's vast, uncharted interior opened up to human development. Rather, the project is the foundation of a total change in technological platform throughout the continent, the sine qua non—in combination with a North-South high-speed railroad that cuts through the Darien Gap between Colombia and Panama—of linking up South America with the World Land-Bridge and the vast leaps in science, technology and consequent productivity of labor that would follow.

The LaRouche movement has studied and actively organized for the construction of various South American transcontinental and North-South railroad corridors for three to four decades (see map). Earlier versions of this project date back to the late 19th Century. One proposal was drawn up by the Intercontinental Railway Commission, started by U.S. Secretary of State James Blaine, which employed U.S. Army engineers to survey and project lines tying the United States through to Argentina and Brazil, presenting a completed map of the intended route to President William McKinley in 1898. The strongly pro-American System McKinley commemorated Blaine's plans as the future of humanity, speaking in 1901 at the Pan American Exposition in Buffalo—where McKinley was shot dead in a British-run operation.

The reason the transcontinental rail project did not come up in Xi's public exchanges with Kuczynski, is that the Peruvian President—lifelong Wall Street banker that he is—is inalterably opposed to the project,

South America: Transcontinental Railroad

South America: Topography

Main rail lines
— Existing
═ Proposed

Source: *EIR*

precisely because the bankrupt international elite recognize it for the game-changer that it is.

The transformative impact that the transcontinental railroad will have on the entire continent can be seen in various ways:

• It will drastically cut shipping times and costs from Brazil and other South American countries (such as Argentina) to Eurasian powerhouses like China, India and Russia.

• It will allow for inter-modal cargo and passenger linkages to be constructed with South America's three great river systems: the Orinoco in the north, the Amazon in the center, and the Paraná/Rio de la Plata in the south. These river systems are already navigable significant distances into the continent's interior (the Orinoco less so than the others), and can also themselves be fully interlinked with a series of great projects (canals, locks, dams, dredging, etc.) to create a single, continuous inland water route. (Readers may rightly be reminded of similar great projects and inter-modal linkages, and their game-changing impact on physical-economic productivity, in the United States, Europe, and elsewhere.)

• It will open up two vast areas in South America's interior to intense, high-technology agricultural production: the Brazilian Cerrado and the Colombian-Venezuelan Plains. These projects will allow South America to nearly triple its current levels of food production in about a decade.

• It will create the basis for dramatically upgrading the scientific, technological, and skilled labor concentrations that now exist in the region encompassing southern Brazil and northern Argentina, which *EIR* has referred to as South America's Productive Axis, and for vectoring this potential for the high-tech development of the continent's interior along the rail/industrial corridors under construction.

There are various possible routes for a South American Transcontinental Railroad, including a Northern Route (which only involves Brazil and Peru) and a Central Route (which involves Bolivia, as well as Brazil and Peru). *EIR* has always argued that both the Northern and Central Routes are technically viable, and that both need to be built (see map).

(For further discussion of these and other South American great infrastructure projects, see: "The World Land-Bridge: Rediscovering the Americas," in *EIR*, Sept. 12, 2014.)

—Dennis Small

With the New Silk Road, A New Sense of Optimism in Serbia

Nov. 28—During a just concluded, four-day visit to Serbia, Elke and Klaus Fimmen of the Schiller Institute found great openness and optimism about the potential of China's "One Belt One Road" policy for the region. Academics, representatives of various organizations, and media were familiar with, and appreciate highly the crucial work and record of the Schiller Institute for the World Land-Bridge. One leading academic, who has written on the importance of the New Silk Road for Serbia, stressed that he completely agrees with Helga Zepp-LaRouche, that this is of global significance and a new paradigm.

At the end of the trip, Elke Fimmen gave a lecture on "The New Silk Road: A Regional and Global Peace Policy of Development" in Novi Sad, Serbia's second-largest city, for about 50 students and economics faculty members, organized by the regional association of economists.[1]

For the first time in decades—decades of regional wars, and economic and social destruction—people now see hope for the future. One former politician said that with the Silk Road, Serbia is in a position for the first time in history to use its geographic and strategic location for the good, instead of being ruined by geopolitics for millennia. The outcome of the U.S. presidential election added to this sense of new maneuvering room. In public "voting," published by the media, the

Schiller Institute

A new railway bridge (white bow) under construction across the Danube River at Novi Sad. It forms part of a new, joint China-Serbia-Hungary high-speed rail line from Belgrade to Budapest.

results had been 95% for Donald Trump. For the Serbians, Hillary was the embodiment of NATO aggression. People agreed that with the Trump victory, the war with Russia has stopped for now. There was great interest in the possibility of realizing Glass-Steagall now, and of reshaping the whole economic policy towards real economic development in the United States and worldwide.

Serbia's Role

Serbia has become central to China's approach to the Central and Eastern European region. At the recent Central and Eastern European summit in Latvia, a first visa-free agreement between Serbia and China was signed and will take effect in January, and the National Bank of China will open a branch under Serbian charter starting next year. And final agreements were made for

---

1. At Novi Sad University in June 2001, Jacques Cheminade and Elke Fimmen presented the Eurasian Land-Bridge, the need for a global New Bretton Woods, and the principles of physical economy, as defined by Lyndon LaRouche. During the same visit, a lecture was also given at the prestigious Institute of Economic Science in Belgrade, founded in 1958.

Central Square, Novi Sad.

Schiller Institute

are imported, including from China. Unemployment is still massive, officially around 16%, while real unemployment is much higher. Youth do not have a future, university graduates end up as taxi drivers or tourist entertainers. In the second biggest city of Serbia, Novi Sad, the average income of a waiter is about 200 euros ($213), while the cost of living is 500 euros ($533). Young people are moving to the few cities and abandoning the countryside, but at present, there are no jobs for them in the cities, either.

starting construction now on the Belgrade-Budapest high-speed railway, which will revolutionize the inland rail grid in Serbia as well. At present, the 80 kilometer train trip from Belgrade north to Novi Sad takes almost two hours.

Other projects are also under way: The Smederovo steel plant that employs 3,000 workers, purchased by the Chinese, is about to be modernized, including complementary port development at the Danube, where the plant is located. While the EU has been attempting to impede progress, there is nothing it can do, since all regulations (including anti-dumping rules) have been carefully followed. An industrial park for high-tech firms is planned for Belgrade, possibly combined with a new harbor. In Bor, the development of one of the largest European copper mines, which also produces silver and gold, is planned. In the past 25 years it has never been properly developed. China is thus vitalizing projects and sectors that have been put under privatization for decades and were left hanging in the air as a huge burden on the state budget.

The amount of investment needed to renew the infrastructure is immense, ranging from 30 to 50 billion euros for the capital city of Belgrade alone.

Serbia has been seeking admission to the EU, which allows the EU to put great pressure on Serbia in many ways. Serbia sees the EU as having been a stumbling block for development over the past fifteen years. Not only have no projects been financed, but EU membership has been constantly delayed. Hundreds of thousands of Serbians have had to live and work in Germany since World War II. Serbians are fed up with the empty promises. Now, either Germany and other EU governments shape up and change course, or they will have lost their chance.

Enforced Backwardness

While annual growth of gross domestic product (GDP) has moved up from 2% to 3% in the last year—which some attribute to the earliest effects of Serbian-Chinese cooperation—industrial production is abysmal, and there is a disproportionately large service sector. Many cheap goods (and not so cheap)

Schiller Institute

Schiller Institute organizer Elke Fimmen speaks on the World Land-Bridge and the New Paradigm, in Novi Sad.

Every Day Counts In Today's Showdown To Save Civilization

That's why you need EIR's **Daily Alert Service**, a strategic overview compiled with the input of Lyndon LaRouche, and delivered to your email 5 days a week.

The election of Donald Trump to the Presidency of the Untied States has launched a new global era whose character has yet to be determined. The Obama-Clinton drive toward confrontation with Russia has been disrupted--but what will come next?

Over the next weeks and months there will be a pitched battle to determine the course of the Trump Administration. Will it pursue policies of cooperation with Russia and China in the New Silk Road, as the President-Elect has given some signs of? Will it follow through against Wall Street with Glass-Steagall?

The opposition to these policies will be fierce. If there is to be a positive outcome to this battle, an informed citizenry must do its part--intervening, educating, inspiring. That's why you need the EIR Daily Alert more than ever.

TUESDAY, NOVEMBER 22, 2016

Volume 3, Number 65

EIR Daily Alert Service

P.O. Box 17390, Washington, DC 20041-0390

- Only Global Solutions, Based on New Principles, Can Work
- Tulsi Gabbard Meets with Donald Trump Regarding Syria
- Robert Kagan Throws in the Towel, Complains U.S. Is Becoming 'Solipsistic'
- War Party Moving To Preempt Trump-Putin Reset
- Syrian Army Makes More Progress in Aleppo
- Duterte Gives OK to Nuclear Power for Philippines
- Europe Will Suffer from Maintaining Russia Sanctions
- Former Chilean Diplomat Confirmed, 'We Will Joyfully Welcome Xi Jinping'
- Duterte and Putin Establish Philippines-Russia Cooperation
- François Fillon, Pro-Russian Thatcherite, Wins First Round of French Right-Wing Presidential Primary

EDITORIAL

Only Global Solutions, Based on New Principles, Can Work

Applying the Principle of Hamilton To Today's Crisis

The following edited interview with EIR's Paul Gallagher was conducted on November 21, 2016.

Jason Ross: I'm very happy to be interviewing today Paul Gallagher, an economics editor of Executive Intelligence Review. Paul wrote the "Frequently asked questions on economics," that we have posted on the LaRouche PAC website. You can find that on larouchepac.com/econ-faqs. This comes up because we have a lot of questions that are coming in about Glass-Steagall, about economics more generally, and took an opportunity to condense and pull them together.

Let me start out by asking Paul the first of these frequently asked questions. You take up something we hear somewhat frequently, where people say, "Well, Glass-Steagall wouldn't have done anything about the financial crisis, because the banks that failed were not combined commercial investment banks anyway, they were just investment banks." What do you say to that?

Paul Gallagher: Yeah, that is the argument that has been adopted from the very top down, including the President, the Treasury Secretary. I think the first thing important to understand is that most people support Glass-Steagall out of a question of justice. Right? That

these really, now immense, many, many, part bank giants have, right up to now, continued to use their power to commit so many immoral and, in many cases, illegal banking practices, from fixing interest rates to fixing foreign exchange rates, to fixing the derivative markets—all of them have been found and have admitted to massive mortgage security fraud, and the list goes on and on, and they are still doing this. As the Wells Fargo episode has shown, it's time to break them up, take that power away from them. That's really what many millions of people understand as necessary and done through Glass-Steagall uniquely...

There is a more serious question involved here,

Bank run on Northern Rock, 2007.

which is what did cause the global financial panic, and that really comes down to really only ten years after Glass-Steagall was finally gotten rid of, approximately a third of the huge deposit base of these very big banks, which is in the range of ten trillion dollars, approximately a third of it, within a decade after the end of Glass-Steagall, had migrated over into securities activities, into broker-dealer activities, into hedge fund owning and maintaining hedge funds. All of the commercial banks, the biggest banks got completely out of their lane over into the lane of securities speculation, the whole casino. So they blew, they puffed up that casino by the fact that they had such a huge deposit base, and they were pulling out of their lane into the shoulder over here, and that meant that when one major financial institution failed, no matter what it was, it happened to be Lehman and AIG, but no matter what it was, they were all going to fail. Because the commercial banks which have our deposits have gotten so far out of their lane into the securities casino.

The major banks are still doing it. They had each, maybe a hundred to two hundred subsidiaries in 1995, the Federal Reserve of New York did a very good study of this. By 2011, each of these giants had three or four thousand subsidiaries, rather than one or two hundred; all these little offshore securities units, special purpose vehicles, derivatives contracts, bets, etc., and that's what the deposits were going into…

We have got to have Glass-Steagall, and we are completely uninterested in preventing investment banks from failing. It might be useful if a number of them and a lot of their individual units were to fail. That is not the concern of restoring Glass-Steagall; it's putting the banks that handle the mass of deposits, the

GLASS-STEAGALL

SEPARATE LEGITIMATE COMMERCIAL BANKING FUNCTIONS *from* SPECULATIVE 'INVESTMENT' FUNCTIONS

BANKS

Under Glass-Steagall standards, all banking institutions are forced to choose between either commercial or investment banking.

Productive functions of banks are federally protected and insured, while other worthless, speculative activities are left out to dry.

New *Glass-Steagall* *Bill*

DERIVATIVES
EXOTIC INSTRUMENTS
MBS's and CDO's
CARBON SWAPS

INFRASTRUCTURE
LOANS TO SM. BUSINESS
MORTGAGES
PENSIONS

TRASH

SPECULATIVE ACTIVITY **IS THROWN OUT** *while* **COMMERCIAL & DEPOSIT BANKING IS PROTECTED**

LPAC

commercial banks, putting them back in their lane, which is providing credit to households, businesses, individuals, revolving credit in the form of auto loans, credit cards, mortgages, this sort of thing, and preventing them from getting out of their lane into unsound banking. That is what the preamble of the original Glass-Steagall Act said.

Financing an Economic Revolution

Jason Ross: On the subject of moving forward, on creating an economic recovery, because a large part of the vote we just saw with the presidential election was a vote in opposition to the destruction and the lack of vision of the Bush and Obama Administrations and the threat of that being continued under Hillary Clinton, in this context, LaRouche has written what he calls Four New Laws to Save the USA Now, which is an appendix in the book Hamilton's Vision, which includes Hamilton's four major economic writings. In that report, Mr. LaRouche says that, given the breakdown crisis we are facing internationally, there are four specific cardinal measures which must be taken. One, Glass-Steagall;

two a system of top down and thoroughly defined national banking, three, the purpose of that credit system is to generate high productivity trends in improvements in employment as through increased energy flux density application in the economy, and fourth, the adoption of a fusion crash program, to reach that next level of economic power seen in the potential of the nucleus through nuclear fusion.

In the context of this, and the idea of saying let's get some growth, let's get some projects going, the *New York Times* published a front page article on November 18th. The article is called, "Trump sized ideas for a new Presidency; build something inspiring." It goes through how Roosevelt built a lot of things, they are still with us today; in contrast the Obama Administration's stimulus program left no program any one can name, nothing is really happening. It says that by investing in things like rail, etc., airports and things like this, that Trump could create an economic recovery.

The New York Times says that, since interest rates are low, the best way to finance a public works program would be for the government to borrow most of the money from investors. Is that the best way to finance a public works program? Since interest rates are low, is it possible for the government to simply borrow money in a standard way to pay for these projects? Would that work?

Gallagher: Now it wouldn't. I have to say I don't really know what they mean by borrowing a trillion dollars from investors. The way in which—the model of what they are indicating might be the Reconstruction Finance Corporation of Franklin Roosevelt, which certainly was successful over a twenty year period of time, which borrowed about fifty billion dollars over that period of time, from the American public. These were not in any way deals for private investors to set up vehicles; rather the Treasury simply borrowed dedicated Treasury Bond issues for the Reconstruction Finance Corporation to engage in all of the New Deal support that it did, and that amounted to fifty billion, perhaps in our current dollars, five hundred billion [dollars].

We need ten times that much investment in new infrastructure. We can get into that a little bit more, in terms of what we really need it to be, and what its character really needs to be, this new infrastructure that is being discussed now, but that amount of borrowing straight out in a short period of time against an atmosphere in which, since election day, the long term inter-est rates are already rising pretty fast, the Treasury bond ten years interest rate has already gone up from about one and three quarters percent to almost 2.4 percent in almost two weeks. That's a really rapid increase, and that was just at the very idea that an incoming Trump administration was going to spend a lot of money, both on defense, increased military spending and also infrastructure.

I'm not at all convinced that that is what the Times means, to simply borrow a trillion dollars from the public by the Treasury, from the international public, because Treasury securities are sold to countries all over the world, but that would be very difficult to do now without there being very rapid increases in the interest rates, and no one in the Times coverage here gives any suggestion of how it would be paid back, or how the debt service on this borrowing would be handled. Alexander Hamilton's voice is always in your ear, saying that public debt is a public blessing if the means for its extinguishment have been definitely provided, which is certainly not the case here.

That's also not the case with the plan that has been circulated by a California professor and a New York billionaire who may become Trump's new Commerce Secretary; that plan is also quite unworkable. What we have to compare it to is the method of generating credit for increased productivity that Alexander Hamilton pioneered, invented, essentially, because that method was used over and over again—John Quincy Adams with the second National Bank; Abraham Lincoln with the greenback policy in the 1860s; Franklin Roosevelt with the Reconstruction Finance Corporation. This method continued to be successful and accounted for the waves of really new infrastructure over the course of the nineteenth century and the middle part of the twentieth century, which really made this country the pre-eminent industrial and scientific power.

We had productivity increases in the most developed measures of productivity from roughly 1935 to 1965, which have never been equaled since the 1870s. That was under the impact of the New Deal, the credit measures necessary to build up the military for World War II, the actual manufacturing investment strategies which the Roosevelt Administrations carried out in order to mobilize the US economic power, which won World War II, and then the Kennedy Apollo Project centered investments in new infrastructure and in new capital investment in industry. These things produced a wave of very rapid increases in productivity through

wikipedia

Chinese high speed train leaving Shanghai's Hongqiao Station.

working of atmospheric ionization in order to bring atmospheric moisture from the ocean over the land and cause it to fall.

That is one example.

We need a 25-35,000 mile national network of high speed rail. We have no capability now of building that. We need to be building a moon colony, and NASA doing all the preparations as other countries are doing only on the drawing board, but would like to collaborate with us, in order to really go back to the moon in preparation for exploration of the solar system—and also potentially to find materials and fuels which are entirely absent here, like helium 3, which are there on the surface of the moon. We need to generally expand NASA, which, after all, is a transportation infrastructure program, right? It happens to be our transportation to get human beings out into the solar system.

the middle decades of the twentieth century. There hasn't been anything like that since.

Ross: You have also pointed out that even if everything the *New York Times* proposed was financed somehow, it is aiming far far too low. This amount of a trillion dollars—you have pointed out that China is already spending that much money, but the US needs far more than that. What would a real recovery look like? What ought we to be doing in the United States?

Gallagher: We could get into a lot of detail on that, which we don't have time for, in terms of individual industries, but to give one example, or to give several examples and then to zero in on one, we need a new water management and water creation infrastructure for the entire western half of the continent, which everyone knows but tends to look away from in a policy sense. The whole western part of the United States, and Canada, as well, are in constantly advancing drought, verging on desertification, and there is no sign of that drought being alleviated, perhaps for decades into the future. These include the most productive areas of the country, California most notably. Water has to be provided both by a really modern, well designed system of moving it from the places that it is falling in great excess, like Alaska and northwestern Canada, and also creating it by desalination, particularly nuclear desalination all along the coasts in that western half of the continent, and by the more advanced and experimental methods which seem to be

We have to increase the power generation capacities of the United States by a great deal; we have to make big changes in industry. But if you look at just the high speed rail component of it, China, in ten years, has put into operation a national network which is still growing rapidly and which is already 12,000 miles of high speed rail. Japan has also shown the capacity to build it very rapidly. We don't have that capacity at all, not currently. We don't have the capacity either to provide the power to a nationwide system of electrified high speed rail—the transformer systems, the pantograph transmission either to the car, to the engine, if it's high speed rail, to the track if it's maglev rail; we can't produce that. The justification of rails over long distances, with extremely tiny tolerances needed in order to handle trains travelling at really high speeds, we don't have the ability to produce those; we haven't even started on it. Clearly, for some of the absolute necessities that we need, we want to turn and collaborate with the countries, particularly China, which are already doing them, and doing them better than they've been done anywhere else in the world; those are the kind of infrastructure investments.

In this *Times* article, by contrast, the biggest thing they were suggesting was a high speed rail line in California, and another one from Washington DC to Boston.

That's not the kind of thing that will really revive the US economy or the productivity of the labor force in the US economy.

National Banking

Ross: Let me switch to some of the questions we have been getting from our supporters, our organizers, some of the questions that came in on You-tube over the last couple of weeks. A number of people asked about national banking and the Federal Reserve. They said, how can we have both the national bank and the Federal Reserve? What will end up happening with the Federal Reserve? Let me

CC0

Greenback from 1861.

put two questions together and see what you think. Another question that came in was about the question of money, about Lincoln's greenbacks, debt free money, is this a meaningful concept? Does this have any relevance to what we have to do today? What can you say about national banking, the Federal Reserve and money?

Gallagher: Let's keep it simple; let's say what Alexander Hamilton did to create the first national bank and to make it successful, among other things to produce the earliest investments in what was then new infrastructure, particularly canals, ports, roads, and also the experiments in rapid manufacturing technique development which Hamilton was himself in the middle of, particularly Paterson, NJ, Hamilton Township, these were places where new manufacturing techniques were being developed, very skilled artisans from European countries, particularly Scotland, were being imported, literally, by Hamilton's agency in order to spread the best techniques in European manufacturing into the United states.

How did he do it? He took the debt, there was the famous argument, which he won, whether the United States should honor all the debt of the period of the Articles of Confederation, the Revolutionary War debt, the debt of the new states. He did assume it all; the Treasury did assume it all. The way he did it though, was to have it invested over a period of time into a new Bank of the United States, which took in this debt, much of which was not being paid, but it was debt for which the United States now had responsibility. It took in this debt, made it its capital, and exchanged it for much longer term, what we would call now preferred stock in the new national bank that Hamilton asked

Congress to create, and they did create, on the basis of his report.

He then had a bank which was capitalized which also had the support of certain foreign lenders, particularly Dutch banks who organized the five million dollar loan to capitalize this bank; he also made sure that the tax income necessary to guarantee the interest on that debt was passed. They were new taxes, particularly on spirits, on liquor, and there also were new revenues of the post office, and that was the basis on which Hamilton saw already, when he first wrote to Congress about what are we going to do with all this debt, and many people were saying, the important thing is to try to pay the principle, why don't we just discard the interest, why don't we just say, we'll write it down, or we'll pay very little of it or no one will care about it. Hamilton said the interest is the important part. If you can replace that debt with much longer term principle, and make sure that you actually pay those interest rates, that you provide the means to do that with taxation, then you can expand what was previously merely debt into a much larger amount of investment capital being deployed by that bank, and that is how he did it.

In 1816, after the war with the British, the Quincy Adams administration realized they needed that bank again, it had been allowed to lapse, so they drafted the Second National Bank, exactly the same method and structure. In 1841 the Congress passed a third national bank, after Andrew Jackson had become furious and done away the second one. That was vetoed but very shortly after that Abraham Lincoln found a way to do that in the beginning of the Civil War, which essentially made a new national banking system, rather than simply a national bank, by tying all of the banks in the new Federal system around the country to a new issuance of US debt, which again was over a long period of time, in which these banks had to buy, hold and actually hold at the Treasury, as part of their of their capital in order to be part of the national banking system.

Lincoln created a national banking system, and on that basis printed greenback currency which was tremendously successful in terms of not only what the war required, but all of the other things which followed—the transcontinental railroad, the state college system around the country, the steel industry, all of the things which made us a first power by the end of the century came from Lincoln's banking reforms and greenback policy.

National banking now would simply mean that, in effect, holders of treasury bonds, this is not new debt, but bonds the treasury has already issued in recent years, the holders of those bonds, which of course include some foreign countries that hold a great deal of it, would be offered the opportunity to place those treasury bonds into a new national bank for industry and for manufacturing and infrastructure as its capital. In exchange for that, those bond holders would have the opportunity to get, instead, longer term preferred stock, essentially, in a new national bank, whose purposes included this kind of real frontier infrastructure that we were talking about.

The means of paying the interest, which would have to be higher than the current zero interest rate environment—which has really been a very destructive one for the economy, for the banking system—the means of paying the interest, although the Treasury would be guaranteeing the long term debt of this new national bank, the bank would have to pay it and would have to have the means to pay it, either in a new tax or by the assignment and perhaps increase of a current tax to the bank, as its income. Then the bank of course has to have working capital, has to have funds, not simply stock but funds to initiate, to lend to initiate these projects, and that it could do either by using its stock and discounting it at the Federal Reserve, in other words getting the Federal Reserve to effectively loan the bank money against the stock that it had, or better, if holders of a trillion dollars worth of treasury debt take that opportunity and place it in the new national bank as capital, and in exchange take the long term preferred stock of this bank, then the Treasury, if it's a trillion dollars, the

Treasury is then in the position to print a trillion dollars in treasury notes.

That is what a greenback is. That is how the Lincoln policy worked. Those treasury notes would go to that bank and be used as its funds for setting all of this investment in motion. And again, since we need, particularly, the new Silk Road, the investment policy, the development and infrastructure policy of China in particular in building all of this infrastructure along the New Silk Road, since we need to join that, it is an ideal circumstance that a trillion dollars in existing treasury debt is held by China. Another trillion is held by Japan, which is the world's number two infrastructure building power and close behind China, and those two are ideally in a position to invest their holdings of treasuries in this new national bank for manufacturing and infrastructure, and therefore to become not only cooperating builders of what we have to do, but also become cooperating issuers of the credit, and we would be cooperating with them also in issuing credit for infrastructure projects outside the boundaries of the United States, because some of the greatest of these projects, like crossing the Bering Strait and connecting high speed rail in this continent to high speed rail in Asia, obviously requires the cooperation of several countries, and it requires these kinds of things, these kinds of things require the cooperation in credit and funding of several countries as well.

This bank becomes the connection to the Asian Infrastructure Investment Bank, the Silk Road Fund, the BRICS Bank, the other new international credit agencies which have been created by the BRICS, particularly by China, in order to get this kind of really big project done.

Ross: When you brought up the creation or assignment of an existing tax as the way to make good on the bank, on what Hamilton had done with the public credit in assigning a definite income stream which would make the interest payments and make the debt secure, it made me want to ask you about—well the Tennessee Valley Authority paid back its loans by selling electricity and things like this. The administrator of the TVA, David Lilienthal, in a book he wrote about his experience with it, asked, "Did the TVA pay for itself"? Yes, it very directly did that by generating fees and income that way, but, he said, even if that had never happened, just the increased income tax in that region of the nation

TVA's Ocoee Dam No. 3, on the Ocoee River in Polk County, Tennessee, USA, 1948.

as a result of the TVA, that would be enough to pay for the project as well. What I was wondering about is, does this put this financing, the use of a tax, does this make it possible to finance projects that otherwise people might say on a project-by-project basis, "this won't directly make money and therefore it would be off limits." Does this enable that?

Gallagher: This is why, in the article I just wrote for the *Hamiltonian*, I attacked user fees, because these kinds of great projects do not pay for themselves in a short period of time. The TVA eventually made a profit over an extended period, but that was never its purpose. And the purpose of a new national bank for infrastructure and manufacturing now, is not that that bank should make a profit over any short term or even decade, fifteen year, twenty year period of time. It's that productivity, throughout the economy, throughout the labor force be raised, which obviously will be accompanied with—everyone understands that that will be accompanied by considerably more tax income generally, and that is how the national purposes of the country are met.

I think what Lilienthal actually said in that final report was that the purpose of the TVA was to pursue the national interest of the United States. It happened eventually to make a profit, but that was not its purpose and that's not the purpose of a bank like this; it simply must be put on a sound basis for a relatively long period of time as having the income means to actually keep its debt sound, to pay the interest on its debt, to keep its debt sound. That cannot be based on user fees. If you

have such a bank and you say it's going to be paid for by user fees, then immediately its managers will want to do the smallest—the way I put it in the article is, "Kennedy said we do these things because they are hard. We go to the moon, we send a man to the moon, we bring him back in this decade, we do these things not because they are easy, but because they are hard."

These are the major new infrastructure platforms we need to develop with this bank. If you have a bank that depends on user fees, it will do things that are easy. It will build or upgrade an airport here or there, it will put up a rail line only in the most crowded, most used corridor, between Washington and Boston, at best. It's going to build a new bridge that has tolls, and so forth. It's going to try to build a water project that immediately can generate water fees. It is not going to do what Kennedy said, these things that are hard, which actually make America a greater and more productive economy than it was before, because those kinds of things that are hard, as he called them, they don't produce this kind of flow back of revenue to the lending agency which provides the credit for it, or in that case to the Congress, which was funding NASA every year. It changes the economy; it transforms the economy, and the result is it's a bigger, more productive economy and there is more income. So NASA, the Apollo project and associated things, as has been well established, paid back to the economy ten to fifteen dollars to every dollar that was spent on it, but it didn't pay that back to NASA, it was an effect on the economy as a whole.

Hamilton simply said, this is what we are aiming for; he knew absolutely: the goal is productivity. His goal was new manufacturing techniques, advancing the productivity of agriculture as well as the rapidly spreading manufacturing capabilities, and that the bank could make that possible but the bank simply had to assure its investors that it was going to make their investments sound. For that, as he said, the means of extinguishing those debts have to be provided in the bank. And they have nothing whatsoever to do with the projects that will be carried out. A liquor tax had nothing whatsoever to do with the new roads and ports and canals and so forth that were built.

Ross: Right! I think this makes the point that there are objectives, or an opportunity to increase productivity, there are levels of social advancement that are only possible with the national involvement in the economy that way, not with individuals trying to make a profit.

Gallagher: Like the TVA. You can look at poverty maps of the United States, and of course the southeast quadrant of the United States has the worst poverty rates. If you look at a map by county of the United States, you see an area carved out of the southeast where the poverty rates are much lower, and that is the TVA. It's still the case. So it was not only that it transformed water management over that whole area, power production, rural electrification, and all these other things, but also libraries, it also raised up the living standards of the population in that area which were the lowest in the country at that time.

The New Global Paradigm

Ross: Let me just ask as a final question to summarize or wrap up as you see fit on the international question. You had brought up earlier we could not build a high speed rail even if we wanted to. You mentioned some of these other—the New Development Bank, the Silk Road Fund, the Asian Infrastructure Investment Bank—how will the US coordinate with these institutions? How are we going to fit in?

Gallagher: Well, it is fundamentally the policy of China and Russia, but in terms of capabilities both for building and for financing it is overwhelmingly the policy of China which has made what they call a "win-win" whole series of offers to countries all over Latin America, all over Asia, many countries in Africa, and that has become associated with the policy of the BRICS, or more particularly of China, India and Russia. This New Silk Road and the corridors across Eurasia which China has initiated the building of, this constitutes the potential for a global recovery from what has been extremely low growth of the whole world economy in the last decade or so, and most especially the absence of any growth in Europe, the absence of any growth in the United States.

Clearly there has to be collaboration in an effort of putting productivity back into the American economy, or putting the drivers for productivity back in,

there has to be cooperation which is being offered now for several years by China in particular—join the Asian Infrastructure Investment Bank. Obama said no, tried to get everyone else out of it, everyone else went into it, but they are going into it, particularly the European countries, with very small contributions to the capitalization. If it is a question of the United States, how will we collaborate in that kind of rebuilding of whole new infrastructure platforms across Eurasia and in this country ourselves? We have no credit institution which is ready to collaborate on that in any way. We have the poor Export-import Bank and nothing else.

We have needed, number one, a complete policy change, getting Obama out of there. We have at least the indications from Trump during the campaign that he had an idea of big investments in infrastructure, an idea of restoring Glass Steagall, so there are indications of a change in attitude toward Russia and China, we'll have to see. But what we absolutely must have in order to make that kind of cooperation is a national credit institution like the ones China has been using in order to drive this development.

Even in recent weeks, three different countries in Ibero-America have upgraded their relations with China on the basis of major investments that its banks are making in those countries' development. They do this because they have major credit institutions, some of them in partnership with other countries, some are Chinese government banks. They have the basis for that credit underlying in the large foreign reserves that they have. We need to start by having such an investment vehicle ourselves, a national investment vehicle in the United States. Then it's very easy, as in the Marshall Plan, to link that vehicle to national credit institutions in many countries, and beginning by linking it to those of China and of the BRICS. Then we can both fund things here, jointly fund third country projects, and combine the joint issuance of credit with joint building because those countries are so far ahead of us, in recent years, in terms of the productivity of the way they have developed their infrastructure so rapidly.

Ross: Great! I think that's a pretty comprehensive view of many of the economic questions we are facing now. Thank you for being on the show today Paul.

Gallagher: Thank you!

A Moment for Greatness

by Kesha Rogers

> The dignity of man into your hands is given. Its keeper be. With you it sinks, with you it will arise.
> —from Schiller's poem, "The Artists"

Adapted from an oral presentation to the meeting of the Manhattan Project, Nov. 26.

Nov. 27—During a recent discussion with leaders of his U.S. national organization, Lyndon LaRouche made the following assessment in response to the rapidly developing global situation. He weighed just how this profound moment of great achievement and profound responsibility must be approached, as it confronts all thinking Americans and all others throughout the world who seek a more prosperous future for the whole of mankind.

"The things to be considered are deep," he said.

They are not choices of program policies; they are not superficial. That goes to the space program, and once you look at the space program in a critical way in terms of the universe—not in a practical way, but in terms of the universe—then you really begin to see what the chances before us in the world now are. Understand that practical interpretations will not cut the mustard. You have to get at the idea of what the procedure is, the manner to create the new universe of mankind.

So, that is the question at hand. What is the procedure that must be put forth to create the new universe of mankind? I think that is the question before us: How do we bring this new universe into existence?

That's the challenge that all of us have right now, as we see the rapid transformations in the world economy. At this very moment, the United States has a unique responsibility to join in the efforts for the global shifts now under way.

What we accomplish in the next four weeks will be decisive for shaping this new universe which mankind must bring about. The imperative fight before us is for the immediate implementation of Mr. LaRouche's Four Laws, with the reinstatement of Glass-Steagall banking protection as a first measure. Mr. LaRouche has defined these Four Laws, not as a part of some sort of policy decision, but as a total transformation, which is now underway, to bring the United States up to the standard of what it must do in light of the global shifts taking place throughout the world. These shifts themselves have been a response to the leadership of Lyndon and Helga Zepp-LaRouche over the past decades, against the evils of a financial oligarchical system; that is what Glass-Steagall represents.

We are now poised to bring down the Bush/Obama/Cheney apparatus—the disintegrating financial system and evil empire—once and for all.

Xinhua/Ding Lin

Chinese President Xi Jinping meets with his U.S. counterpart Barack Obama in Lima, Peru, Nov. 19, 2016.

A Leap in Progress

Once you do that, what is it that you're going to be bringing into existence? I think it is important to look at the developments, the rapid transformation that has been underway for the past several weeks now. Look particularly at the ongoing developments coming from the leadership of the BRICS nations—Russia, China, India, Brazil, South Africa—and particularly from the leadership of Russia and China. This is not something that just sort of fell into our laps, or that should be looked as a development of new events. It is really a transformation of mankind. It is mankind taking a leap in the development of a new system of relations among nations, throughout the planet and throughout the universe, which has to be understood in a critical way.

The conception of mankind, and of the intrinsic nature of mankind, as Mr. LaRouche has identified it, is imperative for understanding the ongoing global events. If, for example, you look at the global shifts manifest in the developments at the APEC summit in Lima, Peru, Nov. 17-19 and the role of China's President Xi Jinping and others there, you see that you have to address this from the understanding that a new system of international relations is now coming into being.

In the aftermath of the summit, President Xi visited Peru, Ecuador, and Chile. China's Foreign Minister, Wang Yi, described the tour as aimed at building a community of common destiny. He told the Xinhua news service that the results were "impressive, making enormous strides towards building a community of common destiny with other nations of Latin America and the Caribbean by holding the higher banner of a peaceful development and cooperation." He said they were coordinating their development strategies, upgrading their cooperation, and bringing benefits to their people.

In the midst of these rapid international developments, our leadership was also manifest. On the opening day of the APEC summit, November 17, Mrs. La-Rouche addressed a meeting in Lima, Peru that had a profound impact. This is really characteristic of the leadership shown by Mr. and Mrs. LaRouche. She addressed the XXIII National Congress of the Association of Peruvian Economists. At the conclusion of the event, the economists issued a conclusive statement of endorsement, saying, "We share Helga Zepp-LaRouche's perspective on world development."

What is under way here has to be understood as a leap in the progress of mankind. We are now at a point where the evil of a system of empire, of degeneracy, of financial collapse, is now totally disintegrating and is ending. This result has been the ongoing work of Lyndon and Helga Zepp-LaRouche and our political organization. This is exactly what Mr. LaRouche addressed yesterday as the fight that is now under way, saying that these are not just choices of programs or policies that can be enacted in a superficial way, or that you can look at these world developments in a piecemeal way. As if this event is happening here, or that event is happening there.

It is imperative to recognize that a new definition of mankind is now coming to fruition. In addressing LaRouche's conception of a corresponding economic platform for this new definition of mankind, my colleague Ben Deniston of the LaRouche PAC Basement Team took up the profound conception that has been uniquely identified by Lyndon LaRouche, that the platform must be conceived from the standpoint of the development of the Solar system, with the leaps necessary for our development of the Moon as a first priority.

'Infrastructure' Not the Answer

But why is all this necessary? How do you think about these things? First of all, you have to ask the question as Mr. LaRouche did:

> What is the intrinsic meaning of the human being? Of the existence of the human being, and of all human beings? What makes the universe do what it does for the function of mankind as such? The question is, what mankind can do to change the behavior of the universe as such.

As he was making those comments, it reminded me of President John F. Kennedy, when he proclaimed, "My fellow Americans, ask not what your country can do for you; ask what you can do for your country. My fellow citizens of the world: Ask not what America will do for you, but what together we can do for the freedom of man." If you really want to address that goal in the way that Kennedy intended, and which the financial British imperial system and oligarchy have completely opposed from the very beginning, you really have to address it from the standpoint of mankind's unique role in changing the behavior of the universe as such.

That means we have to go to work to understand what the characteristics of the universe are, to understand the creative nature of mankind in being able to

President John F. Kennedy (left) visits Mercury's Flight Control Area a few days after John Glenn's flight in February 1962. Glenn and astronaut Alan Shepard are to Kennedy's right.

NASA

increase the leaps of development and transform not just our single planet, but the entire universe. I think that gets at the core of the "platform" conception of economic development of Mr. LaRouche. What Ben Deniston laid out yesterday were the fundamental practical applications that are absolutely necessary to get us to the point where we reject the notion of limits to growth and reject the notion that there is a budgetary crisis that keeps us from accomplishing these goals of mankind in mastering the development of space. We must understand the concept of leaps in economic platforms so that we can avoid addressing the needs of space development from a piecemeal standpoint.

The United States must enter into the new paradigm that is now underway and is being immediately defined by the nations of Russia and China. We have clearly defined the actions necessary to bring the United States into that new system of international relations in our publication, "The United States Joins the New Silk Road: A Hamiltonian Vision for an Economic Renaissance." It outlines the programmatic approach of our movement.

You cannot create an economic renaissance, or even have a Hamiltonian vision for an economic renaissance, by addressing economic development from the standpoint of infrastructure. This gets to the very core of the discussion currently under way. What is the difference between piecemeal steps of infrastructure development, and the conceptual understanding of creating an economic renaissance through leaps in mankind's creative progress?

Mr. LaRouche has taken up that subject on many counts. In a moment I will read a quote from him that addresses it from the standpoint of physical economy: increases in the creative potential of mankind, and the leaps of economic progress that come from these advances in the creative potential of the human mind. I am referring to advances in what we as a species have that is uniquely different from all other species.

When you talk about leaps in economic platforms—my colleagues and I were just discussing this today—it probably would have been mind-boggling to people in the pre-Lincoln era of the Oregon Trail if they could see where we are today. Then, it took four or five months to travel from Missouri to Oregon under very harsh conditions. Now, because of leaps in transportation technology, you can make the trip in a matter of four to five hours.

Then you look at what it took for us to get to the Moon with the Saturn V rocket. That technology—as essential as it was at the time—would not be sufficient now to get us to Mars safely—in the context of the necessary leaps in economic, scientific, and technological platforms. We have to actually develop the region of low-Earth orbit and the region of the Moon, as a platform for launching to Mars. This is something that really has to be taken up.

Higher Conception of Human Identity

Let's go back to LaRouche's conception of an economic platform in physical economics. What I am going to quote from—and I recommend that you go back and read it—is the book that Mr. LaRouche wrote in 2008 after his famous economic forecast of July 25, 2007. It's called *The State of Our Union: The End of Our Delusion!* In that programmatic work, he writes:

In physical economy, for example, it is those creative powers of the individual human mind associated with the means by which the human mind generates, or replicates either a discovery of a universal physical principle, or a modification of the application of that physical principle as such, which is the essential marker of cognitive activity. This includes discoveries respecting the principle of life itself. It is the processes of discovery of such principles, of amplification of the categories of application and range of application of such discovered principles, which are the core subject of creativity. (p. 100)

San Diego Air and Space Museum Archives

Krafft Ehricke, known as the father of the Atlas, here demonstrating his model of the Atlas Space Station.

So, that is what is at hand right now for our understanding of the embodiment,— what lies at the foundation of Lyndon LaRouche's Four Laws. They represent a transformation in the prevailing conception of who we are as a species, and state the corresponding policy that must be enacted now. This is not a policy that can be *eventually* adopted, nor can we wait to see what President-elect Donald Trump is going to do.

Our role and responsibility is to shape the institution of the Presidency and to shape the new Presidency. That means not just shaping relations within the United States and within the process of political activities in the United States. Understand this as a process shaping the universe as a whole, shaping the global developments of the world as a whole, and that is imperative *now*. There is not a choice in the matter; this is not just a nice idea. It has to be undertaken immediately! We have to now realize the Hamiltonian vision for an economic renaissance. There has to be a new conception of mankind underway to do that.

We go back to Mr. LaRouche's emphasis on development in space as a key to how we address the needs of mankind on the planet, how we address this higher identity of who we are as a species. He continues to bring up the role and leadership of the great space pioneer Krafft Ehricke, who has become a dear friend of mine in this fight to understand what is required to lead this nation from the brink of despair, under the evil and destructive policies of the Bush/Cheney/Obama regime, which now has to be ended.

Ehricke's Insight

I want to read a quote from Ehricke's article, "A Case for Space." It is phenomenal, because he writes this eight months after the launch and landing of the Apollo 11 mission. This is February 1970; the Apollo mission had landed in July 1969. It's really fascinating just to think that Krafft Ehricke was not just an engineer, aeronautical scientist, and engineer who looked at space from the standpoint of practical applications. He looked at development in space from the standpoint of the human creative process; we do not go into space because it's there, he wrote, but because we need its potential and we need to develop its potential for the development of the human species as a whole.

On March 25, 1961, President Kennedy had announced the program to land a man on the Moon and return him safely to Earth before the decade is out. There was then a major fight by the limits to growth, anti-human, anti-scientific progress, budget-cutting people, who were prepared to do everything to make sure that it didnt happen. After the horrific events in 1967 that halted the space program—the cabin fire that killed all three crew members of the Apollo 1 mission—there was a two-year period when it was very uncertain

NASA

Astronaut Buzz Aldrin on the Moon on July 20, 1969, during the Apollo 11 mission, the first spaceflight that landed humans on the Moon.

whether we were going to accomplish that goal that Kennedy had set into motion.

But as soon as that goal was accomplished and we had succeeded in "sending a man to the Moon and returning him safely to Earth," despite a major (and continuing) fight, Ehricke wrote this paper, because the budget-cutting, imperialist, anti-development agenda was rearing its ugly head as never before. In his "Case for Space," Krafft Ehricke writes:

Among the many important challenges of our time, space is the only major challenge that is not borne out of past acts of ignorance, indifference, or man's inhumanity to man.... Space opens new horizons beyond Earth and offers

new beginnings in the ways we can manage this precious planet. It offers noble aspirations, opportunities for creative action, for bringing the human family closer together and contributing to a better future for all.

After further developing this thought, he identifies some of the attacks on the space program: Why would we want to spend this money in going into space; we have poverty and so many other concerns, so why would we want to actually spend the money to go into space? Ehricke writes that you do have to deal with war, with poverty, and all of the things that confront the nation and confront mankind; and he says,

Like the space program, these other efforts have important positive goals—badly needed in the era in which loss of identity is feared by so many young people, though never with less justification if they would just tune in rather than out.

He continues,

Improving living conditions and education, conquering disease, and overcoming social injustices are positive goals. The national space activity contributes to many of these efforts and certainly does not impede the others.

Ehricke understood that the inspiration and development of mankind's purpose to enhance our development in space is absolutely imperative for accomplishing these goals, for addressing these concerns confronting mankind. Because they are not concerns that cannot be addressed; you have to look at what is bringing such injustices about.

Mankind has suffered under a limitation on its creative potential. A limitation on growth has been put on mankind. Until we remove that limitation, we will never be able to address these concerns. To remove those limitations, we must define mankind's true purpose: What is the intrinsic nature of mankind? How do we create this new universal system? It is accomplished through the development of space and through bringing forth the vision, once and for all, of a true economic Renaissance in which the development of space is at the core of that mission.

Leap to the Moon

The Epoch of Mankind's Future in Space Has Finally Come

by Benjamin Deniston

Nov. 28—What will NASA's focus be under President Trump? Rather than comment upon ongoing speculation and rumors, let's focus on what needs to happen to secure mankind's prosperous future in the Solar system.

What should the goal of today's space program be? We certainly want to accomplish inspirational and exciting goals—sending mankind back to the Moon, getting people to Mars, and pursuing greater robotic exploration of other planetary systems are all worthy goals now being discussed.

However, there is another, higher, consideration which must guide our actions now: *will the accomplishments we make provide the platform to support qualitative leaps to even greater capabilities in the future?*

Today's space policy should have a generations-long vision to develop the capabilities that will then enable mankind to regularly perform tens or hundreds of the types of missions that we currently see as single flagship missions today. For reasons discussed below, an international mission for the development of the Moon is the clear first step.

Natural Human Progress Comes in Leaps

Yesterday we cheered with excitement, watching NASA's Curiosity rover make its first explorations of Mars; tomorrow we should have more advanced rovers exploring many more planets and their moons (Venus, Mars, Titan, Europa, Enceladus, Io, Triton, Ganymede, Pluto, and more). A few decades ago the world was

CC0

gripped by seeing mankind set foot on the Moon; a few decades from now we should witness mankind exploring other planets with relative ease. We must look to interplanetary space travel, exploration, and development, just as mankind looked centuries ago to transoceanic travel or transcontinental travel—voyages that start as risky and expensive exploration missions led by a handful of brave individuals must become increasingly common occurrences for increasingly large fractions of the population. This will take a few generations to accomplish, but ultimately it is the correct perspective needed to guide our actions today.

In the beginning of the 19th Century, Lewis and Clark risked life and limb to traverse the wilderness of the American continent, achieving something that the average retired RV enthusiast of today can accomplish in a span of a week, or the average airline traveler can accomplish in a day. In the middle of the 20th Century, a handful of astronauts were the first to brave the cold vacuum of space in mankind's first trips to the Moon, achieving what will be common a century from now.

Is space travel more difficult than early transcontinental expeditions? Yes, absolutely—but every new challenge is always more difficult than the last; this is the nature of human advancement.

The question to ask is: how does mankind change extraordinary, singular achievements into ordinary, common activities? The unique and incredible into the regular and indispensable? What enables mankind to uniquely make such dramatic shifts? The answer is provided by Lyndon LaRouche's science of physical economics.

LaRouche's Physical-Economic Platform

During this transition period, leading into the new Trump Presidency, it is critical to raise the level of discussion to the right basis. We can have exciting missions, we can have inspiring missions, but the question to ask is: Are we going to have a program where the investments are going to be the basis for creating a whole new level of activity, that will allows us to do orders of magnitude more than we were able to do prior to that investment? Is this going to create what Mr. LaRouche had once defined as a "physical-economic platform"?[1] Is this going to create an entirely new platform of activity, of potential—of infrastructure, of energy-flux density of technologies—which comes together to support a qualitatively new level of potential activity for mankind?

That is the issue we want to put on the table right now. This goes directly to the vision of Krafft Ehricke, the early space pioneer who worked very closely with Lyndon and Helga LaRouche in the 1980s. Ehricke was one of the leading space visionaries, who outlined in great detail the initial basis for mankind advancing to become a species that dwells in the entire Solar system.

The real understanding of what qualitative revolutions in infrastructure systems mean for mankind's continual creative progress is not connected to the way most people use that term. A better representation would be to think in terms of advancing "platforms" of human development. Go back to thousands of years ago, when the dominant cultures were trans-oceanic maritime cultures. What you began to see, with the development of inland waterways, inland river systems— such as what Charlemagne was doing during his reign in central Europe in developing these canal systems and river systems—was a qualitative revolution above what

NASA

Krafft Ehricke with a model of an orbital hospital.

had existed prior, with these trans-oceanic civilizations. The development of these inland waterways defined a new platform of activity that supported a qualitative leap in what civilization was able to accomplish.

The next leap came with the development of rail systems, especially trans-continental railroads, typified by what Lincoln had spearheaded with the trans-continental railroad across America. Transcontinental rail systems, and the new energy flux-densities provided by the coal powered steam engine, created a new platform, supporting the development of the interior regions of continents for the first time (opening up vast new territories for development) and providing a new space-time connectivity for the economy (enabling new flows of goods, production processes, and higher levels of overall productivity for the labor force).

These trans-continental rail systems defined a qualitative increase in mankind's "potential relative population density," as LaRouche has developed that metric for understanding the science of economic growth. It made things that were at one point incredibly expensive or challenging or risky, become just day-to-day regular activities.

How will we create a similar shift with respect to mankind's relation to the Solar System? What are the key technologies, energy flux-densities, and infrastructures of a Solar system physical economic platform?

Solar System Physical Economic Platform

Even if not discussed in the same terms of reference, the basic elements of a Solar system platform have been well known since the work of Krafft Ehricke and his colleagues. For convenience here we can identify three critical categories of focus.

• **Access to Space**—Because of the massive energy requirements to overcome Earth's gravity, it has been said, "Once you get to Earth orbit you're halfway to anywhere in the solar system." Speaking strictly in terms of energy requirements, this is absolutely true (for example, the Apollo program's Saturn V rocket used far more fuel simply traveling from the Earth's

1. See the Sept. 24, 2010 international webcast with Lyndon LaRouche, "The New Economy," *Executive Intelligence Review*, October 1, 2010.

surface into Earth orbit than it used traveling the quarter of a million miles from Earth orbit to the Moon). Today it costs $10,000 to put one pound of cargo into Earth orbit with rocket launch systems. With current efforts to lower costs, traditional rocket flights to Earth orbit might be cut down to one tenth of present costs (at best). However, new technologies provide far better improvements. What NASA defines as "third generation launch vehicles" and air-breathing rockets can reduce the costs to between one-tenth and one-hundredth of current levels.[2] With advanced versions of these systems, astronauts could ride a space plane taking off from an air-

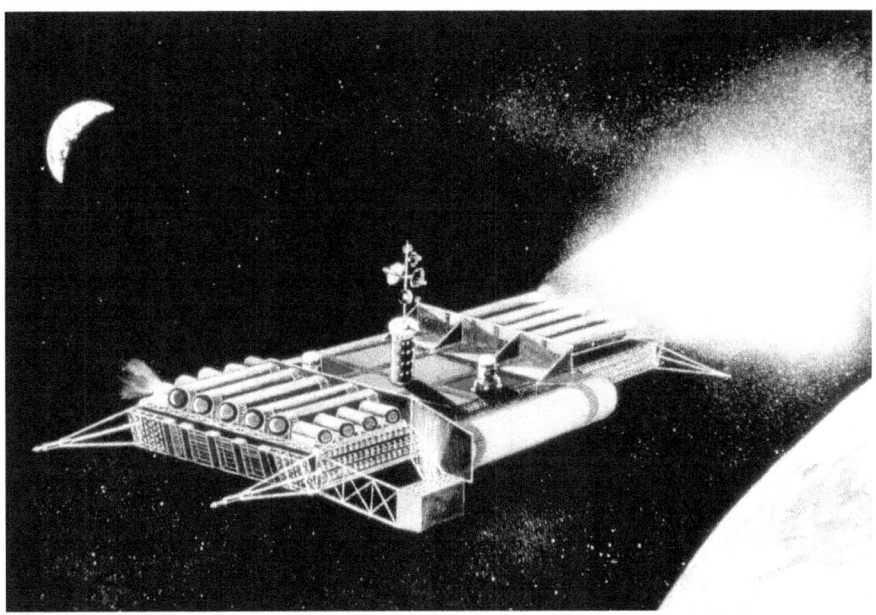

Krafft Ehricke

Painting of a nuclear freighter for industrialization of the Moon, by Krafft Ehricke.

port runway and traveling all the way into Earth orbit.[3] Going further, magnetic-levitation vacuum-tube space launch systems could reduce the costs to merely 0.2% of current levels, making low Earth orbit as accessible as international travels.[4]

• **In-Space Fusion Propulsion**—The energy released by nuclear reactions is an amazing one million times greater than chemical reactions (per mass). For example, the energy contained in the Space Shuttle's 3.8 million pounds of chemical fuel (in its two solid boosters and its liquid fuel tank) could be matched by a mere ten pounds of nuclear fuel. When one grasps the vast distances involved in travel through the Solar system, it becomes clear that deep space travel without nuclear power is as silly as travel across a continent

without fossil (chemical) fuels—it may be done to a limited degree, but it does not support the necessary platform level of activity. Fission, and much more importantly fusion, propulsion are critical to fast and regular access to other planetary bodies. While today's trips to Mars require months of travel time, fusion propulsion can put Mars weeks, or even mere days away.

• **Space Resource Development**—The development and utilization of the resources available beyond Earth will lift mankind above self-supplied excursions into space, to the level of an active organizing force in the Solar System. The ability to develop the resources available on the Moon, asteroids, Mars, or any potential destination in the Solar System reduces the extremely costly requirement of bringing everything from Earth, and begins the grand process of creating self-sustaining systems of economic activity in space, providing needed goods to space activities, and even back to Earth. In addition to the most obvious sources of water, oxygen, and hydrogen, a major focus is a fusion fuel which is nearly completely absent from the Earth, but covers the Moon's surface, helium-3. Advanced (aneutronic) fusion reactions powered by helium-3 could propel spacecraft around the entire Solar system, and power the Earth for centuries to come.[5]

2. See NASA's "Advanced Space Transportation Program" webpage, https://www.nasa.gov/centers/marshall/news/background/facts/astp.html

3. For example, the British company Reaction Engines Limited has designed a spaceplane, the Skylon, powered by their Synergetic Air-Breathing Rocket Engine (SABRE). The U.S. Air Force Research Laboratory has been also been developing a spaceplane design which would utilize the same SABRE engine, and China's Aerospace Science and Technology Corporation (CASTC) is pursuing their own spaceplane designs.

4. See "Maglev Launch: Ultra Low Cost Ultra/High Volume Access to Space for Cargo and Humans," 2010, by James Powell, George Maise, and John Rather (http://www.startram.com/). China's Southwest Jiaotong University is working on similar designs under a project led by Dr. Deng Zigang.

5. See "Helium-3 Fusion: Stealing the Sun's Fire," by Natalie Lovegren, *21st Century Science & Technology, Special Report: Physical Chemistry* (2014).

Taken together, technological and infrastructure breakthroughs in each of these three categories combine to create a new physical economic platform that will completely redefine mankind's relation to the Solar system—as railroads and steam engines had transformed mankind's relation to the continents two centuries earlier.

Destination Moon

Done properly, a mission for the development of permanent basing and manufacturing operations on the Moon can be the best driver program for the creation of a Solar System physical economic platform. The Moon's close proximity makes it accessible for development, and its unique helium-3 resources can provide the fuel for fusion propulsion in space (and fusion power back on Earth), as well as defining a driver program for the development of space mining, processing, and manufacturing capabilities. New space launch systems will lower the cost of Earth-Moon transport, and dramatically increase accessibility to the entire Solar system.

And the world is already looking in this direction. Both China and Russia have their sights set on the Moon, with many of these objectives in mind, and the head of the European Space Agency has put Europe's support behind international development of the Moon.

In a recent discussion with Lyndon LaRouche, he stated, "Your starting point is Krafft Ehricke." And Krafft Ehricke's industrialization of the Moon is the critical driver program that can get a lot of this going. We have helium-3 on the Moon; that puts fusion directly right there on the table. You're talking about developing industrial capabilities and mining capabilities on the Moon. If you're serious about doing this, you want to increase our access to space from the Earth's surface. So, it is excellent that we're seeing a lot of discussion about the Moon coming on the table again; but I think the issue is, are we going to pursue this Krafft Ehricke vision for a real industrial development?

For President Trump it seems clear that the Moon is the obvious choice. The question is whether this will be the beginning of a new, transformative platform that will qualitatively raise mankind's capabilities to an entirely new level. Will this initiate the next revolution in mankind's continual creative advance in the Universe? It is the full comprehension of that question which is required at this time.

Hamilton and Russia: What Broadway 'Rap-ists' Will Never Understand

by Renée Sigerson

Nov. 28—Even in daily conversation, people will commonly compare earthquakes with political revolutions. Earthquakes can be massively destructive, mainly because humanity still has a primitive understanding of why they occur. Revolutionary upheavals, on the other hand, can be either destructive or beneficial. The outcome entirely depends on the morality and depth of devotion of the men and women who lead them.

Alexander Hamilton had a perfected grasp of the difference between social change which produces a progressive advancement of mankind's condition, versus the kind of vicious outpouring of corrupted rage, which leads societies into chaos and violence. The former type of social upheaval dominated the 1776-87 American Revolution because of the moral quality of a small handful of guiding patriots; the 1789 French Revolution quickly became a madhouse of bloody chaos, bringing on an 18-year period of violence under Europe's first continental dictator, presaging the Twentieth century's two global wars.

It is because of Hamilton's deep understanding of these differences in human mindset that he undertook to promote Shakespearean Classical drama in New York, the city he adopted to form a seed-crystal of a better, upward-developing civilization in the Americas.

Virtually all "certified" biog-

creative commons

Statue of Alexander Hamilton by Horatio Stone in the rotunda of the U.S. Capitol.

raphers of Hamilton have failed to investigate seriously this aspect of Hamilton's life. Or, more to the point, though some have noticed relevant "facts" indicating Hamilton's role in establishing New York's Park Theater as an upgraded forum for Classical drama, the academically approved biographers of Hamilton shut out this aspect of Hamilton's life before the living drama of his activities is allowed to come upon the stage.

The reason is that the Park Theater emerged, in a most unforeseeable sequence of events, as the venue which shifted the relationship of the fledgling United States to Tsarist Russia, an irony of living history which William Shakespeare would well have enjoyed.

The following summary account of this effect of Hamilton's efforts, including what happened after he took Aaron Burr's bullet, can only unfold in a manner mirroring the unfolding of a Classically composed musical fugue.

Russia and America

Some elements are known in detail; others are fleeting contrapuntal reflections of the overall dynamic which fly away without a concluding exposition. The relationship between voices creates new ideas. Yet, there remains a unity in the living whole which points towards the basic point: going all the way back to the *common root* of the founding of the United States; the effect of Peter the Great's "modernization" of Russia under the influence of Gottfried Wilhelm Leibniz; and the long struggle of an educated, scientific circle of Russians who came to craft Russia's development, and wanted the United States to be a successful partner. In particular, Russian patriots, largely assembled around forming a state-of-the-art navy, desired the United States to become a *continental* Republic, extending from its Atlantic coast beginnings all the way to the northern Pacific, to join with Russia against the madness of the dying, financier-based European oligarchical powers of western Europe in Britain, France and Spain—the corrupt combination which later emerged as the bloody British Empire.

For many decades, English-speaking academia has labored under the key-and-code that any fact or evidence illustrating the desire of representatives of pre-Bolshevik Russia to cement cooperative friendship with the newborn, revolutionary United States, must not be allowed to come to light. Though the facts proving this to have occurred are readily available, the code has enforced a procedure whereby all evidence of that type is hurled down an unlit, dark corridor, which is then sealed off by a carefully bolted door. If academic researchers desire to have comfortable careers, such "bread scholars" make sure to shut that door closed once they have deposited disembodied facts in the dark beyond.

Recently, the Office of President Vladimir Putin knocked on that door. In the Russian-issued public statement summarizing Putin's first-ever phone conversation with U.S. President-elect Donald Trump, that Office's statement read: "Both leaders noted that next year, it will be 210 years since the establishment of diplomatic relations between Russia and the United States, *which itself should encourage a return to … mutually beneficial cooperation.*" [emphasis added]

In the following account, we respond to that critical

Peter the Great

reference to 210 years past. We push that sealed door ajar, and cast a stage light onto a living drama that covers the period from Hamilton's resignation from the post of Treasury Secretary, to the election in 1824 of John Quincy Adams as U.S. President. During that timeframe, a pro-American grouping within the Russian "intelligentsia," moved to make America an allied friend against their common enemy: the French madman Napoleon Bonaparte, and his secret supporters among the British financial scorpions who hated the United States and wanted Hamilton killed. German patriots associated with "Poet of Freedom" Friedrich Schiller played an important role in this period as well.

Among the objectives of this Russian grouping, aimed at securing a better direction for all of mankind's development, was the desire to foster America as a powerful *continentally ensconced force*, comparable to the vast terrains under Russian rule. The idea was to lead mankind out of the insanity—which still exists today—whereby a financial jetset located in a few cities could "rule the world" by creating octopus-like tendrils engaged in financial skullduggery, slavery, drug trafficking, and fomenting war, wherever their naval outposts could reach. Thus emerged the idea both in Russia and America, that the interior zones of nations had to be developed to enable mankind to reach a higher level of purpose and discovery of the principles of organization of the physical universe.

To prevent this aspect of America's actual evolution from becoming known, the financial elites have been spewing out venom against Russia going all the way back to the proverbial "day one" of the founding of the United States, often justifying their denunciations by nurturing moles within Russian society to spew hatred against the United States.

There is little new in tone or content to London-Wall Street-owned western press attacks on Vladimir Putin, that hadn't been hurled against Russia as early as 1815, if not before.

Hamilton's Theater Project ended up having a role in bringing Russia and America closer together. In reaction against this process, one of the key actors in our account was assassinated, his death marking one of the pivotal downturns in modern civilization. But by situating the facts of the matter as we do here, we aim to reverse a tragic development, and turn mankind's flaws toward a discovery of the sort of penitence which frees human beings to mobilize new qualities of creative life. And, of course, this, in fact, is the sacred intention of Classical drama, entirely distinct from the silly, Jacobin ravings currently distracting Broadway in the form of a spectacle misnamed "Hamilton."

William Dunlap

also became stage director, and finally manager of the firm. OAC had been a favorite of General George Washington, who attended their performances when living in New York. Founded in the 1750s, OAC was a collection of emigré English and Irish actors, who came wandering to the Americas looking for settlements where theater had not been banned by the colonial governments, or in some cases, the Puritans. When Washington attended, theater was still banned by the Continental Congress as a morally seditious activity. (Thankfully Friedrich Schiller issued his famous essay in 1782, "Theater As a Moral Institution," in which he demonstrated the morally *necessary* role in society of the Greek chorus and Classical drama in enabling human beings to discover their own potentiality for creativity and the Good.)

In this environment, it is not surprising that the English actors who attempted to bring Shakespeare to America had rather dissolute personalities. Dunlap was surrounded by back-biting egotists, who were constantly stealing money from the firm and arguing with one another about who would get the lead role.

Working with Hamilton, a completely new financial design for bringing Classical drama to the public was created. One hundred thirty shareholders were recruited from professional New York households and the circle of Hamilton's friends, and seasonal tickets were issued, which Hamilton and his wife Eliza always purchased. Dunlap advertised in London to recruit new actors, and negotiations were launched to exchange better actors from a Pennsylvania theater group. This resulted in Thomas Abthorpe Cooper, a serious English actor whose performances of Hamlet had left Philadelphia audiences in stunned admiration, moving to New York.

The opening night of the Park Theater, which was in a new building with better staging, featured Shakespeare's *As You Like It*, and a brief encore called *The Purse*. Nonetheless, due to cultural backwardness, bad weather, and fears of yellow fever, the new drama com-

And So, the Curtain Rises

In 1795, Alexander Hamilton resigned as Treasury Secretary of the United States, though he continued to direct President George Washington's cabinet out of his law firm in New York. Among his new clients, he admitted William Dunlap, a portrait artist turned Classical stage director, whose drama group, "The Old American Company," was chronically bankrupt.

New Jersey-born Dunlap was one of many American youth sent by their parents to London to study under American portrait artist Benjamin West. The largely self-taught West was so acclaimed that even during the American Revolution, the British Crown kept him in service, while American youth came to benefit from his knowledge. Among those youth was the 14-year-old John Quincy Adams, whose letters thanking West for taking him on a tour of London museums while his father handled diplomatic negotiations with the Crown, are still today readily available. The shared influence of this experience has relevance for the entire process described.

In 1785, Dunlap returned to America, taking up residence in New York, where he was determined to become a stage designer. The quixotic Old American Company (OAC) accepted his application, and soon he

The Park Theater was New York's first world class entertainment venue.

pany still failed to achieve financial solvency.

That is, not until 1798, when an unforeseeable change occurred which had much broader implications.

The shift occurred as two apparent coincidences unfolded, actual events for which there is no proof that they were intentionally related. Shall we say: they were a "sign of the times." And those times were deeply affected by the fact that Europe was being plunged into massive armed conflict as the man-beast Napoleon Bonaparte was amassing his military power.

Hamilton and Washington were always concerned that Europe's wars would spill over into the new, vulnerable Republic, as had already been threatened during the 1793 Whiskey Rebellion. Hamilton had a visceral disgust for that sort of Jacobin anarchism, and his support for introducing Classical drama in New York aimed at using a Classical renaissance in that Hudson River-based port city, as the center for allowing all Americans to become much more educated and politically responsible for the "posterity" of the nation.

The first apparent coincidence occurred after Hamilton, in 1797, issued the controversial pamphlet known as "The Mrs. Reynolds Affair." More has been written about this item, whose release may well have been a mistake on Hamilton's part, than on any other aspect of Hamilton's life. As known, in the pamphlet he admitted to earlier, discontinued involvement in an adulterous liaison, which undoubtedly had been a political setup against him.

As the pamphlet stirred political gossip throughout New York, in 1798, Thomas Abthorpe Cooper handed to Dunlap a manuscript which contained a translation of a play which had taken the European continent by storm. The author of the play was Weimar, Germany-born August von Kotzebue. The original text was in German, but the author was also known as the protected favorite of Russia's Empress Catherine II, who had approved this young German writer's appointment to run her St. Petersburg "German Theater."

Titled in English *The Stranger*, but based on the German original *Menschenhass und Reue* (roughly: *Misanthropy and Remorse*), the play portrayed the case of a young woman who has secluded herself in a permanent state of penitence for the guilt of having committed adultery. Considering the intensity with which Hamilton's political enemies reacted to his pamphlet, it is hard to imagine that the following had no effect on public reaction at large.

In the final scene of *The Stranger*, which is carefully prepared by the author, the lead character delivers a penitential soliloquy, identifying with painfully developed insight that flaw within herself that caused her to fall victim to a criminal seducer. Her proven transformation provokes her estranged husband and grief-stricken children to rush into her arms with forgiveness, and throughout Europe, no matter the language in which the play was performed, audiences would respond to Kotzebue's concluding breakpoint with tremendous outpourings of emotional sympathy, sobbing and wailing, to the point of howling to show their support for the main character's proven remorse for her sin.

Dunlap decided to stage the play. After reading the script to the cast, he noted in his diary, "I never saw a play affect performers so truly before." The performances in New York elicited the same quality of explosive emotion as had earlier occurred in Europe.

Moreover, Kotzebue had awakened within the American-based acting troupe a deep interest in what was then called "the new German theater." He was, by far, no equal to the leading dramatic writer operating out of Weimar, namely Friedrich Schiller, nor the most influential shaper of German cultural policies, Johann Wolfgang von Goethe. But, reflecting his early childhood fascination with pro-American German philosopher and playwright Gotthold Lessing, Kotzebue was able to capture on the stage the precise emotional and intellectual conflicts of his average contemporaries, and to provoke them to rethink in the social environment of the theater, their own follies in a way that captured, intently, their imaginations.

Beginning with *The Stranger*, Park Theater performed 18 plays by Kotzebue over the coming two years. For the first time ever, the theater had stable financial support. Kotzebue became nearly a craze within the population of New York, and the playwright wrote a letter to Dunlap thanking him for the publicity.

New York's *Commercial Advertiser* newspaper noted in March 1799: "To see something from the pen of Kotzebue is now the general wish." In 1799, Park Theater performed his *Count Benyowsky; or, The Conspiracy of Kamtschatka*, the tale of a prison camp revolt in Siberia, under the command of a Polish captive who was also a supporter of the American Revolution. Soon, Kotzebue became not just a New York, but a nation-wide early-American theatrical craze. By 1815, *Count Benyowsky* was performed in Baltimore at the official celebration marking the victory of the United States against Britain in the War of 1812—the same event which featured the debut of John Stafford Smith's setting of Francis Scott Key's "Defense of Fort McHenry" under its new title, "The Star-Spangled Banner."

Kotzebue knew he was inferior to the greatest playwrights. But he churned out 300 plays addressing contemporary topics, including Britain's slave system in Jamaica, portraying a slave family in completely human, ordinary terms before virtually all-white audiences. He was primarily a journalist, and yes, an agent of influence of the Russian patriots with whom he was associated; yet as we document below, he was really something more. He became linked in the view of many nations to the works of Friedrich Schiller, the true genius in drama of that time, giving people in many language-cultures an access-point to study Schiller in the original language. In England, where German progress in science and culture forced the introduction of German language studies, students were known to say, "Schiller and Goethe are for reading; Kotzebue is for

August von Kotzebue

the stage."

The fact that this man embodied an exchange of culture and of national aspirations between Russia, German intellectuals, and the United States, was considered very dangerous by the imperial masters of old Europe. In 1819, Kotzebue was stabbed to death by a deranged student. In the next phase of our examination, we see how the staging and eventual burial of any reference to Kotzebue after his death, set the stage for nearly two hundred years of demonization of Russia. Once he was killed, Kotzebue's murder was used by an imperial alliance between Britain and Austria's Hapsburgs to create the myth of Russia as the monstrous dictator of all Europe.

Russia and the Next Phase

We may never know if the actor Cooper suggested performing *The Stranger* to Dunlap in order to blow apart misguided public preoccupation with Hamilton's case. Yet, whatever the verdict on that matter, the second coincidence in this period of time, is that while all of this was occurring, future U.S. President John Quincy Adams had been named, following his assignment to conclude the controversial Jay Treaty with the Netherlands, as U.S. Ambassador to Prussia. As the assignment allowed him a lot of free time, Adams engaged in intensive study of the German language and theater, testing his skills as a translator of "the new" poetry and attending German theater in Berlin. Thus, both Adams and Hamilton in this period were "on the same page."

This is significant because in this period, President John Adams and his wife Abigail became intense enemies of Hamilton. By the time he was elected, the elder Adams was heard to denounce almost everything Hamilton had been associated with. In contrast, his son worked under Hamilton as negotiator of the Jay Treaty with the Netherlands; supported, as Hamilton did, the U.S. purchase of the Louisiana Territories; and finally, when he became President, supported and oversaw the completion of the Erie Canal which Hamilton had proposed—a project also supported by William Dunlap's

Adam von Krusenstern

continuing work on Classical painting and theater.

So, though Hamilton never lived to collaborate with John Quincy Adams in what he accomplished as U.S. Ambassador to Russia, beginning in 1807—the exact date referenced by President Putin's press release—the following will show that there always existed a thread that linked their work. That thread continued to be influenced by the activities of August von Kotzebue.

Germany's Voice in U.S.-Russia Ties

A concise detour into some further details of Kotzebue's life sets the stage for dramatic, real-life events over a period of 20 years beyond what has been indicated so far, bringing us to the shocking circumstances and effects of his murder.

When hired to head Catherine II's German theater, Kotzebue had legally committed his two sons from his first marriage to be taken as wards of the Russian Navy, to be educated as officers. Their mother having died, he remarried, becoming a brother-in-law of Adam Johann von Krusenstern, soon to be named Admiral of the Russian Navy.

The adventurous complexities of his life brought him to the very inside of the winding corridors where power was wielded in old Europe.

In 1801, Kotzebue returned to Russia from Germany, where he had relocated, to visit his two sons. Immediately upon crossing the border, he was arrested and transported far into Siberia, allegedly under orders of Tsar Paul I, the heir of the deceased Catherine II. In a beautifully written book describing the year he spent in Siberian exile, Kotzebue inserted an unmistakable reference letting it be known that he was to be included as among Europe's "admirers" of America's founder Benjamin Franklin. No other reason is ever given as to why he was exiled.

His petitions to the Tsar, who he was convinced had been misled to imprison him, finally yielded his release. The Tsar—whose own controversial circumstances will not be detailed here—had him transferred from prison to become director of a new museum founded in St. Petersburg. One day, while Kotzebue was working in the museum, in the same building, Tsar Paul was murdered by a circle of conspirators. Kotzebue insisted these were the same conspirators who had originally arranged for his own exile.

During these years, Napoleon rampaged across Europe, looting the treasuries of every nation and demanding troops be amassed everywhere to be put under his command. It is under these conditions that John Quincy Adams was named Ambassador to Russia in 1807, the date cited by Putin's office.

Add to that context: In 1807, Napoleon defeated the Prussian army in the devastating battle of Jena-Auerstedt. Europe was crestfallen by the implications of Napoleon's seemingly "invincible" power. Immediately, a circle of Prussian officers headed for Moscow to join Tsar Alexander I's army. Everyone knew that having crushed Prussia, Napoleon would begin preparations to invade Russia.

Among those Prussian officers was Friedrich Schiller's brother-in-law, Wilhelm von Wolzogen. Schiller himself had passed away from lung disease in 1805, a year after Hamilton was murdered by Aaron Burr. Wolzogen was a dedicated scholar of his brother-in-law's intellectual and artistic accomplishments. By studying Schiller's strategic writings on Europe's 17th-century Thirty Years War, including the dramatic trilogy *Wallenstein*, Wolzogen designed a plan for destroying Napoleon for good whenever he dared to enter Russia.

The period of this interaction between Prussia's

leading military strategists and Russia, is the same period that John Quincy Adams arrived in Moscow as America's first-ever official emissary. During the five years he was in Moscow and St. Petersburg, he had frequent access to Tsar Alexander, but in particular, he communicated with the head of Alexander's cabinet, Count Nikolay Rumyantsev. In turn, Rumyantsev was in continuous collaboration with Kotzebue's brother-in-law, Adam von Krusenstern, on the development of the Russian Navy. Their goal was to match England's command of the seas by carrying out exploratory missions throughout the Pacific Basin. On the first such expedition, which concluded in 1806, Kotzebue's sons Otto and Moritz both served as crew members under Krusenstern's command.

Count Nikolay Rumyantsev

Rumyantsev spoke frequently with the American Ambassador, famously emphasizing how much he admired the United States, even to the point that he desired to retire there, though his health prevented him from doing so. The leading subject they discussed was how to fix the border between America and northern territories claimed by both Russia and England. As Rumyantsev and John Quincy Adams tested each other on the question as to whether Russia or America would assert claim to the mouth of the Columbia River in the Oregon Territories, the Count made clear that whatever the outcome, he represented a pro-American grouping in Russia that rejected the sentimental attachment of other leading Russian circles in favor of England's monarchical system. These Russian patriots *wanted* the American experiment to succeed, and for the United States to have a powerful position on the Pacific Basin to counter the madness of Europe's imperial centers.

In 1809, Napoleon invaded Vienna for the second time, and advanced to position himself at the border with Russia. In the same period, President Madison ignored John Quincy Adams' desperate letters advising him to resist, at all costs, allowing the United States to get into a war with England, since Europe had agreed to make England the leader of its anti-Napoleon "Alliance."

As soon as U.S. gunboats attacked English ships which had been seizing U.S. sailors (a problem Tsar Alexander had volunteered to mediate, as he had successfully done in the past), war was declared between America and England on both sides. The Tsar was compelled to remove Rumyantsev to appease London, and a foolish Count Karl Nesselrode took control over the Russian cabinet.

John Quincy Adams sat out his disappointment, and continued his primary objective: to win Russian support for the best possible arrangements to make the United States a *continental* Republic. The common interest of the two countries was clear. Russia also oversaw a vast, uninhabited terrain. Its borders had to be secured, to allow for the maximum possibility of successful economic progress. For the United States, that meant the northern Pacific border of the United States would have to be that same 48th parallel which had given the United States unlimited access to the iron ore deposits of the area of Michigan. On the Pacific coast, that would mean that the United States, and no other country, could set the rules for navigating the Columbia River.

In those years, John Quincy Adams was therefore deeply concerned with destroying his political enemies in the Federalist Party, from which he had resigned after briefly serving as their Senator, and voting in favor of the Louisiana Purchase. He knew that the so-called Essex Junto, a pro-British faction within the Federalist party, were committed to splitting the United States into rival micro-states. He saw his work in Russia as key to counteracting Britain's role in fostering subversion through the Federalist ranks. He wrote to family members from Russia: "If that [Federalist] Party are not effectually put down in Massachusetts as they already are in New York ... the Union is gone. Instead of a nation, coextensive with the North American continent, destined by God and nature to be the most populous and most powerful people ever combined under one social compact, we shall have an endless multitude of little insignificant clans and tribes at eternal war with one another for a rock, or a fish pond, the sport and fable of European masters and oppressors." And again: "The whole continent of North America appears to be destined by Divine Providence to be peopled by one nation.... For the common happiness of them all, for their peace and prosperity, I believe it indispensable that they should be associated in one federal Union."

Napoleon retreating from burning Moscow.

John Quincy Adams' passionate commitment to the developed unity of the nation as a whole echoes precisely the devotion of Alexander Hamilton in his role as Treasury Secretary and chief aide to President Washington.

Thus, trust and agreement with the Northern Pacific giant Russia, was a prerequisite to ensuring that the United States could both expand in territory, and yet still endure. John Quincy Adams valued enormously the experience he gained living in Russia and building trust with its leaders. At a point when he still hoped to prevent the War of 1812 from erupting between the United States and Britain— as war would then exclude commercial ties and deeper cooperation between the United States and Britain's temporary ally Russia— Adams wrote to Rumyantsev: "I lament the war, particularly as occurring at a period when, from my good wishes for Russia and for the Russian cause, I should rejoice to see friendship and harmony taking place between America and England, rather than discord.... I know the war will affect unfavorably the interest of Russia."

In 1812, when Napoleon massed his forces along the Russian border to invade, the Tsar—under advice from the Prussian circle around Wolzogen (who himself had died in December 1809)—did not attempt to defeat Napoleon's advance, but merely deployed his army to slow it. When Napoleon reached Moscow, a terrible winter had already begun. As advised by their Prussian allies, on the Russian government's command a great fire was set, and the city of Moscow burned to the ground. Its population had retreated to the countryside, its leaders to the northern city of St. Petersburg. John Quincy Adams moved to St. Petersburg along with diplomats from throughout Europe, while "General Frost and General Famine" reduced Napoleon's half-million-man force to fewer than 20,000.

As this was happening, in war-destroyed Vienna Kotzebue contacted the great German composer Ludwig von Beethoven, whose career had come to a halt as war had shut down the musical life of the city. Kotzebue intervened to get work for Beethoven. This collaboration, which began around the time Beethoven first performed his ground-breaking *Symphony No. 7*, then continued until Kotzebue's death. Not accidentally, it was subsequently the Russian nobility which most generously supported Beethoven's writing of his great *Missa Solemnis*, a work the composer dedicated to inspiring humanity to recognize the actual creative nature of the human species. In the manuscript of the *Missa Solemnis*, Beethoven dedicated it to the "inner peace" which allows human beings to communicate "from heart to heart." The first-ever performance of the *Missa Solemnis* was financed by Russian leaders, and occurred in St. Petersburg.

Kotzebue's Assassination

In 1815, Rumyantsev personally financed a new Pacific expedition, commanded by Kotzebue's son Otto.

The expedition lasted three years, and marked a breakthrough in the skill-levels achieved by the navy, as well as the knowledge gained by Russia of the land masses and populations lining the huge Pacific Basin. To this day, the calm inlet bordering Alaska below the Bering Strait, where access to the shore is more manageable, is named Kotzebue Sound, with its central city also bearing that name. The naming was done by the expedition crew in honor of Otto, whose standard of leadership was to treat sailors as well as indigenous people humanely, as had been fought for by American supporter John Paul Jones.

Karl Sand

In 1819, Otto was assembling the materials for publishing an account of the mission, which had traversed the seas from Alaska to the Sandwich Islands and an island which he named New Year's Island (now named Mejit). He was excitedly waiting to give the draft to his father, the experienced journalist, to have August edit it in preparation for translation into many languages. But before Otto could arrive at his father's home, August von Kotzebue was murdered, stabbed to death while standing by the front door of his house, by Karl Sand, an ideologically fanatical youth leader of the 1817 Wartburg Festival, where, in the style of George Soros's "color revolutions," thousands of books were burned by fanatical students. (A century later, the Nazis cited the Wartburg book burning as their precedent.) Assassin Sand tried to commit suicide, but died slowly, during which time he justified his act as necessary because of Kotzebue's attacks on the degenerated youth movements which had assembled under the endless tribulations of war.

Sand's circles branded Kotzebue a "Russian spy." Overnight, Kotzebue was turned into an object of hatred throughout German-speaking Europe. Intellectuals throughout Germany were afraid to denounce his murder, convinced that if they spoke, they too would be targeted next. More important, Austrian Foreign Minister Count von Metternich, upon hearing that Kotzebue was murdered, coldly moved, without any signs of sorrow, to use his death to impose upon Europe a 30-year dictatorship now called the infamous Carlsbad Decrees. His cold and calculated reaction has often been noted with suspicion, as it calls into question whether in fact Sand was being used by an intelligence operation to take Kotzebue out of the picture.

Censorship, imprisonment of newspaper editors, harassment of political dissenters, and scrutiny of religious leaders erupted throughout Europe under the guidance of the Austrian foreign ministry, but with the backup of a morally broken and virtually insane Tsar Alexander I.

The real turning point had been 1815, where for a year, the monarchies of Europe had gathered in an environment of degeneracy and self-adulation for a nightmare called the Congress of Vienna. Rather than allow the defeat of Napoleon to emerge as an opportunity to uplift the suffering populations of Europe by promoting economic progress and an intellectual Renaissance, the bureaucrats and oligarchies of Europe chose to recreate Napoleonic oppression under a new management. For current readers, it is useful to know that the Patriot Act passed after the September 11, 2001 atrocity in the United States, was in its mindless breadth of blind oppression, as well as its diversion from the real causes of terrorism, a replica of that 1819 Austrian Hapsburg Carlsbad Decree gambit.

Suddenly, throughout Europe, Kotzebue was being branded a "bad person," while in some quarters, frightened and dismayed people were praying for Sand as a virtual Saint. The French author Alexandre Dumas included the case of Sand in his famous book series, *Celebrated Crimes*, depicting the social strata Sand exemplified as a socially hostile lower nobility which identified with the medieval fantasy world of knighthood—namely a precursor of Nazism.

And it was not merely Kotzebue who came to be branded and then forcibly driven into obscurity by popular opinion; under the Carlsbad Decrees, Russia as a nation, and its leaders, also were suddenly portrayed as the most evil of all oppressors.

While Metternich ran the secret police apparatus

wikimedia commons

The Congress of Vienna

Prince Metternich

when a crisis hits, is an expression of the game that also developed out of the assassination of Hamilton: never allow the United States and Russia to act upon their common interest, because that will bring to an end the petty imperial power of the London/Wall Street system of murderous financial city-states.

In the surviving 1821 conversation books of the deaf Ludwig von Beethoven, the following exchange appears:

It seems to me that we Europeans are going backwards, and America is raising itself in culture. The present relationship at least is not favorable; the just claims of Americans to independence, on the contrary, support this.

The saddest tendency of this new revolutionary spirit is an egotism poorly demonstrated, or rather too clearly shown. What purpose is gained by the murder of Kotzebue? Although he was no moral luminary in the world, yet he was opposed to many a priest's tale, and would have been again if he were living.

What man is in a position to estimate the results of such an act and consequently consider it as good and necessary?

that selected out enemies to be targeted by legal persecution, the enforcer of this atrocity was identified as Russia. Admittedly, Tsar Alexander was in very bad shape coming out of the workover he had received in Vienna in 1815, and fell generally right into the traps set for him by Britain and Austria. But, relevant to today's situation, the barrage of public attacks on Russia once the decrees were in place, greatly resembles the outpouring of demonization hurled daily by the liberal media against Russian President Putin. Thus, it is not because of lingering Bolshevik hobgoblins circulating in Moscow that Putin is always being attacked; it is because the same psychological shell-game is being played that was unleashed following the assassination of Kotzebue. It is the same shell-game that former Vice President Dick Cheney played the day after the 9/11 massacre, when he called for an invasion of Iraq, a country that had nothing to do with the atrocity.

It is because of this twist from reality, that to this day, Kotzebue is virtually never mentioned, although his murder was used to trigger a 30-year legal atrocity throughout Europe. More important, the reflex of Metternich and his British friends to always blame Russia

The moral frenzy unleashed by the Sand murder was so great, and so deliberately intensified by Metternich, that the world came to be turned upside-down. One religious mentor of Sand's was investigated by police, but then was spirited out of Europe by a leading member of the Boston Transcendentalist Movement and given a post at Harvard University. A professor of philosophy defended Sand's act by saying he was justified in killing Kotzebue because he did it out of sincerity. The latter was briefly suspended from teaching by Metternich's officials, but subsequently given back his post. In this case, the legacy of this professor also led directly to the founding of twentieth-century Fascism.

Fortunately, John Quincy Adams never forgot what he learned about Russia while living there and working with its pro-American advocates. In 1817, Adams was appointed Secretary of State by President Monroe. Britain's Secretary of State for Foreign Affairs, Lord Castlereagh, worked overtime to convince Monroe that Tsar Alexander was about to

The Russian Navy, pictured here, was used by Tsar Alexander II to prevent Europe from interfering in the U.S. Civil War.

invade South America. For years, Adams parlayed between Britain, which begged him to sign a doctrine whereby the United States and Britain together would stand against this Russian threat, and on the other side, the Russians with whom he was still discussing America's northern Pacific boundary line. Old Thomas Jefferson wrongly weighed in and tried to persuade Monroe to work out a doctrine that would unite Britain and America against Russian escapades in the southern Atlantic.

Despite all the evidence that a disoriented Tsar Alexander was indeed becoming more oppressive towards his own people, Adams resisted any alliance with England. He prevailed over Monroe, and in 1823 released a founding statement of American foreign policy: that no imperial power would ever be tolerated by the United States on the continents of the Americas. One year later, he reached his objective, and Russia emerged as the first nation to sign on the dotted line in the what became known as the Russo-American Treaty, agreeing that the northern Pacific boundary of the United States was in fact the 48th parallel, giving the United States control over the use of the Columbia River. In fact, the principle of the Monroe Doctrine was being applied not just to the Atlantic, but also to the Pacific. It was only twenty-two years later that Britain finally agreed to that border. Subsequently, the Russian Navy was used by

Tsar Alexander II to prevent Europe from interfering in the U.S. Civil War, and in 1867, Russia virtually gave Alaska, the northernmost habitable territory on the eastern side of the North Pacific, to the United States, in order to ensure that Britain and Japan would not be able to close in on Russian Siberia.

Americans bend in the direction of tolerating the outlandish abuses hurled at Vladimir Putin, under the influence of experts telling them, "well, this is a revival of the Cold War." But that argument is a fraud. The outrageous and foolish nature of the anti-Putin media wars reveals their origin: the template for the design of anti-Putin propaganda is the outpourings of British Foreign Minister Castlereagh, himself a bloody murderer as the poet Shelley warned, and his cohort Metternich, as they arranged a world of continuous war coming out of the Congress of Vienna. Their intention was to prevent the development of science and classical culture from advancing the cause of cooperation among nation states. This doctrine of hell upon earth was further developed by the early Twentieth century under the name "Geopolitics." All of that evil is now going down the drainpipe of the "juvenile" phase of human history, as a new combination of world leaders assembles around the living legacy of Hamilton, John Quincy Adams, Russian and Chinese statesmen of good will, and Renaissance statesman Lyndon LaRouche.

EDITORIAL

CALL TO ACTION

Germany's Future Lies with The New Silk Road!

by Helga Zepp-LaRouche, chairwoman of the German political party Civil Rights Movement Solidarity (BueSo)

Nov. 26—Heinrich Heine's famous concern comes to mind: "When I think of Germany in the night…"

Indeed, where is Germany headed, or rather, where is it drifting? The fact that Angela Merkel is going to run for a fourth term is not reassuring. Contrary to the impression she is attempting to create, four more years of a Merkel government are no promise of stability, but the opposite.

Both the Brexit and the election of Donald Trump to the U.S. Presidency are expressions of the rejection of the entire paradigm of neo-liberal "globalization," which is just a

oil on paper on canvas by Moritz Daniel Oppenheim (1800—2)
Heinrich Heine (1797-1856)

synonym for the Anglo-American empire. That "globalization" has led to the impoverishment of growing sections of the population, to the benefit of the financial oligarchy, in all countries that have been subjected to the rules of neo-liberal monetarism.

That "globalization"—i.e., the City of London and Wall Street's demand for unipolar supremacy over the world—is responsible for an entire series of wars based on lies, from Afghanistan to Iraq, Libya, Syria, and Yemen, which together caused the refugee catastrophe. "Globalization" also means color revolutions, a policy

of regime change against democratically elected governments such as in Ukraine; it means the eastward expansion and encirclement policy of NATO and the EU, and it likely would have brought us sooner rather than later into a global confrontation with Russia and China under a Hillary Clinton administration.

Chancellor Merkel and the shocked Ursula von der Leyen represent this losing paradigm, and the idea of four more years—with no change in policy and absolutely no vision for the future—does not mean stability, but escalating political divisiveness in Germany and the disintegration of an EU in rebellion. With the next financial crisis, which is bound to come, the Merkel-Schaeuble duo is sure to foist the costs on the citizens once again, and risk chaos by so doing. The fragility of the abominable refugee deal with Erdogan and various governments in Africa, promises that it will only be a matter of time before this crisis again explodes.

Merkel represents this paradigm which is irreversibly sinking. Just like the 304 members of the European Parliament who have just voted for a resolution accusing Russia of conducting massive anti-European propaganda, she supports an EU and NATO policy which does exactly what they accuse Russia of doing. We must put an end to the logic of the Cold War once and for all.

President-elect Trump has said that he wants to cooperate with Russia and China, and has already held conversations with Russian President Putin and Chinese President Xi to this effect. Trump has even signaled that the United States would like to participate in the AIIB and cooperate with China's New Silk Road policy.

In the space of only three years, China's Silk Road initiative has become the greatest infrastructure and economic growth program in history, twelve times larger than the Marshall Plan if measured in today's dollars. Seventy nations are cooperating with it, and more than 30 international institutions. China alone has provided 1.4 trillion Euros in investments; 4.4 billion people are already benefitting from an unbelievably multifaceted array of them—high-speed trains, energy generation and distribution, water management, new science cities, basic scientific research, innovation, joint research for space exploration, and so on. Xi Jinping has offered cooperation with the New Silk Road to every country on Earth on the basis of "win-win" cooperation. More and more countries are swinging into this new paradigm which, instead of being a zero-sum game, helps overcome poverty and underdevelopment for the common advantage of all.

Join Me in This Fight

For more than 25 years, I have campaigned for the program of constructing the New Silk Road, a program which I, along with my husband Lyndon LaRouche, proposed for the first time as a response to the Fall of the Wall and the disintegration of the Soviet Union. We have presented this concept at hundreds of conferences and seminars around the world since then, and now it is the policy of the majority of the human race. With your help, we can now put this program on Germany's agenda—a program which would especially profit the *Mittelstand* (small and medium-sized industry), and from which many productive jobs would be created.

To create a real perspective and alternative for Germany, we don't need an AfD [party] which has no solutions to offer, but, together with me, you can put cooperation with the United States, Russia, and China on the agenda in building the New Silk Road. It is only through such cooperation that we can develop the Middle East and Africa with a New Silk Road-Marshall Plan, and thus solve the refugee crisis humanely. That is, moreover, what General Michael Flynn, Trump's new security adviser, had already called for in April 2015.

Germany must work for this peace policy for the 21st Century, a totally new paradigm which replaces geopolitics with the common aims of Mankind, and must make itself a part of a real "community of common destiny," as Xi Jinping has put it.

Germany must also make an important contribution to the dialogue of cultures, which must accompany this new world economic order if we are to be successful. We in Germany have a rich heritage of humanist philosophy and Classical culture, which, wondrously, find an echo in the highpoints of other cultures. Only if we revive the best cultural expressions of all nations, and bring each other into a living dialogue, can we overcome the current civilizational crisis.

Join me in the fight to ensure that this extraordinary opportunity is seized in and for Germany—an opportunity for cooperation with the new, ready-to-cooperate administration in the United States, and the economic alternative which exists in the New Silk Road dynamic. If you do so resolutely, Germany can again become a nation of poets, thinkers, and inventors [a patriotic German expression: "ein Volk der Dichter, Denker, und Erfinder"], and future generations will enjoy progress once again.